PETER LATHAM

WHO STOLE THE TOWN HALL?

The end of local government as we know it

POLICY PRESS SHORTS POLICY & PRACTICE

First published in Great Britain in 2017 by

Policy Press
University of Bristol
1-9 Old Park Hill
Bristol
BS2 8BB
UK
+44 (0)117 954 5940
pp-info@bristol.ac.uk
www.policypress.co.uk

North America office:
Policy Press
c/o The University of Chicago Press
1427 East 60th Street
Chicago, IL 60637, USA
t: +1 773 702 7700
f: +1 773 702 9756
sales@press.uchicago.edu
www.press.uchicago.edu

© Policy Press 2017

British Library Cataloguing in Publication Data
A catalogue record for this book is available from the British Library.

Library of Congress Cataloging-in-Publication Data
A catalog record for this book has been requested.

ISBN 978-1-4473-3727-0 (paperback)
ISBN 978-1-4473-3729-4 (ePub)
ISBN 978-1-4473-3730-0 (Mobi)
ISBN 978-1-4473-3728-7 (ePdf)

Cover design by Policy Press
Front cover: image kindly supplied by istock
Printed and bound in Great Britain by CMP, Poole
Policy Press uses environmentally responsible print partners

In memory of Ron Stockbridge (former Chair of the Labour Campaign for Open Local Government and leader of Lewisham Council from 1984 to 1985) who died on 15 January 2011

Mick Williams (former Convenor of Democracy4Stoke) who died on 10 January 2013

Peter Gibson (former Croydon Trades Council and pensioners' leader) who died on 16 December 2013

Contents

List of tables

Acknowledgements

I wish to thank Rodney Bickerstaffe for writing the Foreword; Professor Danny Dorling for reading the first draft; Professor Richard Hatcher who sent me his papers on the neoliberalisation of councils and combined authorities; and Professor Patrick Ainley for his support throughout the writing of this book.

Foreword

Developing and updating the themes of his previous publication *The State and Local Government*, the author's new book is welcome and timely not only for the second decade of the century, but for many years to come. The issues and problems examined are not to be resolved easily or quickly, as the last 35 years have proved.

The power of big business and its corrosive anti-democratic and profiteering ways are a huge and continuing challenge. By shining the torch of scholarly, painstaking research and analysis, evidential ammunition and hope is here given to any who care to read or dip into *Who Stole the Town Hall?*.

Local government as a key democratic institution is on its knees. The number of citizens, especially the young, voting (or rather not voting) in council elections is a potent omen. It betokens not only a lack of political education and understanding by and of the electorate, but the distrust, exasperation and anger at the parlous position of local politics and of politicians at all levels.

Lack of service provision, its quality or frequency, and clear postcode and other inequalities, cause disorder, distress and huge anger. Millions are facing inexcusable difficulties and poorer life chances.

Peter Latham's keen analysis nails the reasons for this dreadful situation from the context of his long experience and from his Marxist standpoint, and he makes positive if sometimes necessarily controversial proposals for corrective action.

His intense and wide reading is stamped on each page. He really has done the work for his readers. There are extensive quotations and clear statistics, all underscoring the current state of local government; how we arrived at it; whether or not it can continue as it is; what are the engines of change; and, importantly, what the people can do to make things change for the better.

The book lays bare the purpose and manipulations of the new laws which the Tory-led Coalition government introduced. They encourage municipal burglary and enrich both domestic and international corporate interests at the majority's expense; but neither does the author spare the New Labour years from cogent criticism.

For any interested in knowing more about local government finance, cuts in spending and the replacement of any pretence of community coherence and dignity by privateering greed, there is ample knowledge here. And so there is on the City of London's malign and corrupting influence, US-style elected mayors, and much more. And there are suggestions of real alternative ways to regain local democracy and a better future.

You don't need to be an academic to find this book useful and to appreciate the range of topics and analyses. You just need to care and want to change things for the better.

Rodney Bickerstaffe
Former General Secretary of Unison

About the author

Dr Peter Latham is a sociologist, former researcher on direct labour at the London School of Economics, senior lecturer, lay activist in the former National Association of Teachers in Further and Higher Education and full-time official in the University and College Union. From 1999 to 2006 he was Treasurer and then Secretary of the Labour Campaign for Open Local Government. His previous publications include *The Captive Local State: Local democracy under siege* (2001), *New Labour's US-Style Executive Mayors: The private contractors' panacea* (2003) and *The State and Local Government: Towards a new basis for 'local democracy' and the defeat of big business control* (2011). He is also a UCU delegate to Croydon Trades Union Council; and a member of both the Communist Party of Britain and the Labour Land Campaign.

List of abbreviations

BATC	Birmingham Against the Cuts
BME	black and minority ethnic
BTUC	Birmingham Trades Union Council
CA	combined authority
CEO	Chief Executive Officer
CfPS	Centre for Public Scrutiny
DCLG	Department for Communities and Local Government
DEM	directly elected mayor
ERS	Electoral Reform Society
GLA	Greater London Authority
GMCA	Greater Manchester Combined Authority
GMATUC	Greater Manchester Association of Trades Union Councils
LGA	Local Government Association
LVT	Land Value Tax
MOPAC	Mayor's Office of Policing and Crime
NAO	National Audit Office
NCIA	National Coalition for Independent Action
OBR	Office for Budget Responsibility
ONS	Office for National Statistics
PCC	Police and Crime Commissioner
PCP	Police and Crime Panel
PFI	Private Finance Initiative

PPP	Public–Private Partnership
PWC	PricewaterhouseCoopers
SRA	special responsibility allowance
STV	single transferable vote
SV	supplementary vote
WMCA	West Midlands Combined Authority

INTRODUCTION

My previous book, *The State and Local Government* (Latham, 2011a), analysed developments in the UK – and other advanced capitalist countries and South Africa – plus the south Indian state of Kerala, Cuba, Venezuela and the Brazilian city of Porto Alegre: to show that there are alternative models of 'socialist decentralisation' in local government to neoliberal 'austerianism/localism'.

The introduction of executive government in England and Wales since New Labour's Local Government Act 2000, as Chapter One shows, concentrated decision-making powers in fewer hands. The Local Government and Public Involvement in Health Act 2007, moreover, gave council leaders virtually the same powers as local authority directly elected mayors (DEMs). And in most authorities the committee system was replaced by the cabinet, overview and scrutiny system. Hence most councillors no longer make policy, and feel marginalised, with little influence over issues that affect their local areas, although, since the Localism Act 2011 allowed them to, 13 English councils have reverted to the committee system. Council leaders' powers have also massively increased via the 'payroll vote' of special responsibility allowances (SRAs). Therefore, as the prospect of fewer and lower SRAs may be the main reason why only 13 councils have reverted to the committee system since the Localism Act, Chapter One proposes that no councillors should be paid more than the median gross weekly full-time earnings in their locality.

The privatisation model in the Tory-led Coalition government's White Paper titled *Open Public Services* (HM Government, 2011), as Chapter One also shows, is based on *Payment for Success*, published in 2010 by three senior partners at KPMG (Downey, Kirby and Sherlock, 2010). Councils are also being neoliberalised via new models of local government that prioritise the interests of property developers and big business. The UK outsourcing market is now the second-largest in the world outside the US; and the amount spent by local authorities on outsourced public services almost doubled from £64 billion during the last Labour government to £120 billion during the Tory-led Coalition government. Thus, contrary to the government's empowerment rhetoric, this book argues that the government's main purpose is to complete the privatisation of local government and other public services – started under previous Tory governments and intensified under New Labour – in order to restore the conditions in which profitable investment and capital accumulation can take place.

Public services provide benefits to both individual service users and the wider society. Universal access, delivery according to need, services free at the point of use and delivered for the public good rather than for profit should be at the heart of any model of service delivery. The public sector is best placed to provide public services that meet these criteria and should be the default model of delivery. Chapter One also proposes an overall reorganisation of the structure of local government in the UK to eliminate the democratic deficit whereby it has the highest average population size per local authority in Europe. That is, there should be more councillors and councils – each with the committee system, which is much more inclusive than any other form of governance – covering smaller areas.

Chapter Two focuses on developments since the Localism Act that reinforce the main arguments against directly elected mayors (DEMs), including 'metro' mayors, which the Conservative government is now imposing on combined authorities (CAs) in England. As this chapter shows, DEMs lead to cronyism, patronage and corruption; remove the working class from this layer of local democracy and replace them with a brigade of full-time career politicians; are the optimal internal management arrangement for privatised local government services; create an arena focused on personalities, not politics; have not increased turnout and lack voter support; have an undemocratic voting system; and cannot be removed. Hence this chapter concludes that all types of DEM should be abolished – that is, local authority DEMs, the Greater London Authority DEM, and CAs with 'metro' DEMs, which should be replaced by elected regional assemblies.

Chapter Two also shows that, although the central driver for imposed 'metro' mayors is economic, the devolution of powers to city regions is intended to give credibility to a Conservative discourse of democracy and local empowerment and alleviate hostility to centralised control from Whitehall. It is a strategy aiming to convince working-class voters in the largely Labour-run CA urban conurbations that the Tory party is 'the real party of working people'. These so-called devolution deals, moreover, are all being negotiated behind closed doors. Hence, pending the abolition of CAs run by DEMs and the structural reorganisation of local authorities proposed in Chapter One, this chapter proposes having elected delegates from union, community and user bodies on their boards and scrutiny committees. Meanwhile, pending abolition of DEMs, the single transferable voting system (STV) should be used for all elections, with the right to vote at 16, plus the right of recall leading to a new election if a DEM turns out to be bad or ineffective.

Chapter Three shows that the main arguments against directly elected police and crime commissioners (PCCs) in England and Wales are similar to those against DEMs; and that the Tories now want there to be a legal duty to collaborate for the three emergency services with shared governance for the police and fire services under PCCs. As this chapter shows, PCCs also lead to cronyism, patronage and corruption; are a monoculture that excludes the working class; are the optimal internal management arrangement for a privatised police service; are invisible; have not increased turnout and lack voter support; have an undemocratic voting system; and cannot be removed. Hence this chapter proposes that PCCs should be abolished as part of the overall reorganisation of the structure of local government proposed in Chapter One, in which each local authority would have a police authority made up of elected local councillors, representatives of trade unions and community organisations. Similarly, until abolition, as proposed in Chapter Two, the STV should also be used for all elections, with the right to vote at 16, plus the right of recall leading to a new election if a PCC turns out to be bad or ineffective.

Chapter Four looks at the financial provisions of the Localism Act, subsequent legislation relating to local government finance, recent and future trends in public and private sector employment, trends in UK public expenditure and local government finance in the UK. This chapter also shows that some councils, which have been cut harder than the rest of the public sector, are already becoming financially unviable. The chapter concludes that the council tax, stamp duty land tax and business rates should be abolished and replaced by a system of land value taxation, plus a wealth tax and more progressive income tax to fund increased provision of directly provided public services.

Chapter Five concludes that an alternative economic and political strategy is the pre-condition for implementing the policies proposed in Chapters One to Four and reversing the cuts already made and planned; and that a new basis for federal, regional and local democracy is necessary, for which the labour movement and its allies must win support from large sections of the electorate.

Most local authorities no longer rely solely on 'in-house' operations to deliver reduced services or their own internal functions. Alternative approaches – in addition to outsourcing – include the use of 'shared services' between multiple local authorities and also between local authorities and other public bodies; local authority trading companies; mutuals; and social impact bonds. The latter alternatives are all critically discussed.

The Encarta UK English Dictionary defines 'demise' as 'the end of something that used to exist, especially when it happens slowly and predictably'. Hence – unless present policies are reversed – we now face the prospect of what the former leader of Birmingham City Council, Sir Albert Bore, called the 'end of local government as we know it' (quoted in the *Guardian*, 31 October 2012). Moreover, three years before Margaret Thatcher came to power, in 1976 the Labour prime minister James Callaghan signalled a shift away from the Keynesian post-war consensus and towards neoliberal policies. That is, as Dexter Whitfield (2014, p 7) notes, austerity policies

> did not create a 'new opportunity' to reconfigure the state, nor was it an example of 'shock doctrine'. The financial crisis merely allowed the acceleration of reconfiguration, because the implementation of neoliberal policies in the public sector and welfare state has been systematic and continuous for over three decades. The financial crisis, austerity policies and subsequent recession created new opportunities to advance private ownership, finance and service delivery; freedom of choice through competition and markets; deregulation; the deconstruction of democracy to increase the role of business in public policy making and to consolidate corporate welfare; and reduce the cost and power of labour.

1

THE LOCALISM ACT, OPEN PUBLIC SERVICES AND THE NEOLIBERALISATION OF COUNCILS

This chapter analyses the main provisions of the Localism Act (other than those relating to directly elected mayors and local government finance, which are assessed separately in Chapters Two and Four), the *Open Public Services* White Paper and the neoliberalisation of local councils.

Governance

The Localism Act 2011 – some of whose provisions apply in England and Wales and some of which only apply in England or Wales – received the royal assent on 15 November 2011 and contains provisions for over 100 orders and regulations in addition to its 483 pages, 223 clauses and 34 schedules. Hence, as George Jones and John Stewart – the leading academic critics of the Act – concluded:

> It is ironic that a Localism Act contains so many means by which central government can prescribe how local authority powers are to be used, their procedures developed and criteria to be applied by them ... its development has been conditioned by the dominant

> centralist culture of central government with the result
> that ... *[it] could as well have been called the Centralism Act.*
> (Jones and Stewart, 2012, pp 93–4, my emphasis)

The original Bill would have allowed councils to change their governance systems only after the next local election, which in some cases would have meant authorities not being able to make a change (such as returning to the committee system) for as much as three years after the Act came into effect. But, as a result of lobbying by the Local Government Association, all local authorities in England and Wales operating under executive arrangements may now opt to change their governance arrangements following a full council resolution, which takes effect following the council's Annual General Meeting (Latham, 2015, pp 11–13).

Conversely, there is no requirement in Scotland for councils to adopt a particular political decision-making and scrutiny structure, although eight of Scotland's 32 unitary councils have the cabinet system (Table 1.1). Moreover, in Northern Ireland from April 2015 the Local Government Act 2014 reduced the number of local councils from 26 to 11 'super' councils. This Act provides several alternative forms of governance that a council may choose to operate. These are: a committee system; executive arrangements; and prescribed arrangements. A committee system is the default option, which all of the 11 new councils have (Table 1.1). But councils may choose one of the other methods if at least 80% of councillors present and voting so decide. If a council wishes to operate a different form of governance, instead of either committee or executive arrangements, it may apply to the Department of the Environment, who may prescribe alternative arrangements (NILGA, 2015, p 6).

Why the committee system is not out-dated

The *Local Government Chronicle* on 19 April 2012 gave exclusive coverage to a report by the Centre for Public Scrutiny (CfPS) and summed up its main findings under the headline 'Committee system could now be out-dated, councils warned'. The CfPS takes this view because it considers 'consensus decision-making makes partnership working less responsive' now that 'decisions are made at partnership level, and many services are contracted out, jointly commissioned or procured and delivered in other, innovative ways' (CfPS, 2012, pp 5 and 27). That is, 'partnership working' (CfPS's euphemism for outsourcing and privatisation) is incompatible with 'consensus decision-making' (CfPS's euphemism for policy-making by all councillors). Conversely, as Andrew Coulson (2012) argues,

> committees are much more inclusive than any other form of governance. They give a voice to all the elected councillors, and potentially bring to the table all their talents. They make it harder to take decisions in secret. They give councillors a means of putting into effect the commitments they make when they stand for election, and they keep council officers on their toes because they can never be quite sure what will happen when they attend a committee – even if most of the major changes that might be made to a report will have been agreed in the group meeting of a majority party beforehand. They also allow backbench councillors to specialise, and provide a means to induct them into how council services are run.

Sixteen years after the replacement of the existing committee system with a formal cabinet, overview and scrutiny system, one of the main issues emerging from research by the Association for Public Service Excellence (APSE) is the feeling of disillusionment among non-executive elected members, who feel marginalised from real decision making, with little influence over issues that affect their local areas. APSE found that 65% of executive councillors thought local government modernisation measures had worked well, compared with 37% of non-executive councillors. While 58% of executive members believed separating decision-making powers from scrutiny had increased transparency, less than 30% of backbenchers agreed.

Significantly, two out of three non-executive members thought the modernisation agenda had marginalised their role. The report also suggests that fiscal austerity has dented councillors' belief in their capacity to further improve services. While almost 75% of councillors overall thought their authority was committed to service improvement, 87% of cabinet members believed that they personally could contribute to improvements, whereas only 43% of backbenchers believed they could contribute (APSE, 2015). 'Some would see this as an opportunity to make arguments for a cull of councillors – suggesting that if there isn't anything for them to do then get rid of them'. But as Paul O'Brien, APSE's Chief Executive, also states, 'if we believe that democracy is a fundamental principle of our society then why would we want to slip further down the ladder as one of the most underrepresented countries in Western Europe?'

Hence the committee system – in which all members make policy – is even more necessary now, with severe cuts in services and increasingly complex approaches to delivery mechanisms (including outsourced contracts, arm's-length arrangements and multiple partnerships). Furthermore, some of the problems now emerging in children's services might have been picked up earlier with the committee system; and the overcharging scandals in some outsourced contracts might not have occurred. Moreover, as argued above, this should be part of an overall reorganisation of the structure of local government in the UK to eliminate the democratic deficit, whereby this country has the highest average population size per local authority in Europe (Latham, 2011a, p 72). That is, there should be more councillors and councils – each with the committee system, which is much more inclusive than any other form of governance – covering smaller areas.

Councils that now have committee-style structures

During 2001/02 in England 316 (81%) councils opted for the leader–cabinet model, 10 for a directly elected mayor following successful referendums and one (Stoke-on-Trent) for a directly elected mayor and council manager. Most of the smaller English district councils (59) opted for 'Alternative Arrangements' and the streamlined committee system, which allowed for not more than five policy committees, and four of these by 2007 had shifted to the leader–cabinet model (Latham, 2011a, p 80). The Department for Communities and Local Government (DCLG), in its impact assessment published at the same time as the Localism Bill, estimated that between 17 and 34 authorities in England would change their governance arrangements using the powers in the Localism Act. It also stated that:

> The cost to local authorities of holding a referendum on changing governance models is estimated at £70,000–£250,000 and it is estimated that up to three councils will hold a referendum. The Government does not envisage that those councils choosing to operate the committee system will be subject to any additional operational or administrative costs to those operating one of the executive models ... save for transitional costs. (DCLG, 2011, p 8)

The CfPS – based on detailed case studies of 15 unnamed councils planning to change in 2012, 2013 or later – concluded that around 40 councils in England were actively considering making changes. These did not include the 'core cities' forced to hold directly elected mayoral referendums (see Chapter Two). Meanwhile, during the passage of the Localism Bill through Parliament many commentators had thought that most of the authorities that would take advantage of the opportunity to adopt a committee-system form of governance would be shire districts, in part because of the perceived success of the streamlined committee system in 'fourth option' authorities with populations of less than 85,000. The CfPS research, however, found that only one shire district council was considering a post-2012 change; and – despite the DCLG impact assessment showing that the change would not involve any significant costs – a number of district councils told the CfPS that their lack of interest was due to 'anticipated costs and a lack of benefit from making the change' (2012, pp 1 and 7).

Prior to the Localism Act's coming into effect 79 councils in the UK (the Isles of Scilly, 28 English district councils with 'alternative arrangements', 24 Scottish unitary authorities and all the 26 councils in Northern Ireland) had committee-style structures. By May 2015, as Table 1.1 shows, 77 councils (two London boroughs, three English county councils, four English unitary authorities, 32 English district councils, the Isles of Scilly, 24 Scottish unitary authorities and all the 11 new 'super' councils in Northern Ireland) had the committee system. Therefore, by May 2015 under the Localism Act in England 13 more councils, of which only four were Labour controlled, had reverted to the committee system.

- Two out of the 13 are London boroughs (Barnet, which is Conservative controlled and Sutton, which is Liberal Democrat controlled).
- Three are county councils (Cambridgeshire and Norfolk, which have no overall control and Nottinghamshire, which is Labour controlled).
- Four are unitary authorities (Brighton & Hove, Hartlepool and Reading, which are all Labour controlled, and South Gloucestershire. where the Conservatives have minority control).
- Four are district councils (Newark & Sherwood, which is Conservative controlled, Stroud, which is controlled by an alliance of Labour, Liberal Democrats and Greens, Fylde, which is Conservative controlled and Canterbury, which is Conservative controlled).

In addition, four Conservative-controlled councils have introduced 'hybrid' arrangements: Kent County Council (where each cabinet member has a committee advising him/her on any issues within their remit and all key and non-key member decisions before they are taken); Oxfordshire County Council, which now has Cabinet Advisory Groups; Guildford Borough Council, which introduced two politically balanced executive advisory boards held before each meeting of the Executive and replaced the existing scrutiny committees with one overview and scrutiny committee responsible for post-review of executive decisions and wider external review; and Sevenoaks District Council, which now has five Cabinet Advisory Committees (see Table 1.1).

Why only 13 more councils have switched to committee-style structures

CfPS's explanation is that committee-style structures are incompatible with privatised services. Yet this did not prevent arch-privateers Conservative Barnet Council from reverting to the committee system in May 2014 (see Table 1.1). Moreover, the CfPS fails to acknowledge the relevance of the Local Government Act 2000, which massively increased the power of the executive via the 'payroll vote' of special responsibility allowances (SRAs) and the proportion of full-time councillors, such that in 1998 the annual average allowance in England for leaders (£7,749) was twice the average for backbench councillors (£3,699). By 2008 the average leader's allowance of £23,852 was four times the average for backbench councillors; and the average allowance of £15,809 for cabinet members was three times the average for backbench councillors (Latham, 2011a, pp 82–3).

Nor has the situation changed since 2008. For example, according to Croydon Council's website, the Labour leader in 2015/16 received £55,223 (the basic allowance of £11,239 plus SRA of £41,984), which was 4.7 times greater than the allowance received by backbench councillors. And the nine other Croydon cabinet members – appointed by the leader – received an average allowance of £43,967 (the basic allowance plus an average SRA of £32,928), which was 3.9 times greater than that received by backbench councillors. The leader and the Labour group also control the allocation of 23 out of 29 SRAs. Hence – unless in the forthcoming period a broad alliance is able to win a return to the committee system – members' material interests will ensure that the status quo continues.

Table 1.1: Council governance systems in the UK, excluding the City of London and Greater London Authority

	Committee	Party control	Executive	(Hybrid)
England				
32 London boroughs	1. Barnet[a]	Conservative		
	2. Sutton[b]	Liberal Democrat	30	
36 Metropolitan boroughs			36	
27 County councils	3. Cambridgeshire[a]	No overall control		
		Conservative		Kent[c]
	4. Nottinghamshire[b]	Labour		
	5. Norfolk[a]	No overall control		
		Conservative	24	Oxfordshire[c]
55 Unitary authorities	6. Brighton & Hove[b]	Labour		
	7. Hartlepool[c]	Labour		
	8. Reading[c]	Labour		
	9. South Gloucestershire[b]	Minority Conservative	51	
200 District councils	10. Barbergh[d]	Conservative, Liberal Democrat and Independent		
	11. Barrow-in-Furness[d]	Labour		
	12. Brentwood[d]	Conservative		
	13. Canterbury[f]	Conservative		
	14. Christchurch[d]	Conservative		

14

Committee	Party control	Executive	(Hybrid)
15. Corby[d]	Labour		
16. Craven[d]	No overall control		
17. Daventry[d]	Conservative		
18. East Cambridgeshire[d]	Conservative		
19. East Dorset[d]	Conservative		
20. East Northamptonshire[d]	Conservative		
21. Epson & Ewell[d]	Independent		
22. Forest Heath[d]	Conservative		
23. Fylde[f]	Conservative		
24. Gosport[d]	Conservative		
	Conservative		Guildford[g]
25. Harlow[d]	Labour		
26. Isles of Scilly	Independent		
27. Melton[d]	Conservative		
28. Newark & Sherwood[c]	Conservative		
29. North Warwickshire[d]	Labour		
30. Oadby & Wigston[d]	Liberal Democrat		
31. Purbeck[d]	No overall control		
32. Ribble Valley[d]	Conservative		
33. Richmondshire[d]	Independent and Liberal Democrat		

Committee	Party control	Executive	(Hybrid)
34. Runnymede[d]	Conservative		
35. Ryedale[d]	Conservative		
	Conservative		Sevenoaks[c]
36. South Derbyshire[d]	Conservative		
37. Stroud[c]	Labour, Liberal Democrat and Green alliance		
38. Tandridge[d]	Conservative		
39. Torridge[d]	Conservative		
40. West Devon[d]	Conservative		
41. West Lindsey[d]	Conservative		
42. Weymouth & Portland[d]	No overall control	167	
Wales			
22 Unitary authorities		22	
Scotland			
32 Unitary authorities[e]			
43. Aberdeen	No overall control		
44. Aberdeenshire	No overall control		
45. Angus	SNP		
46. Argyll & Bute	No overall control		
47. Clackmannanshire	No overall control		
48. Comhairle nan Eilean Siar	Independent		
49. Dunfries & Galloway	No overall control		

		Committee	Party control	Executive	(Hybrid)
		50. Dundee	SNP		
		51. East Dunbartonshire	No overall control		
		52. Edinburgh	No overall control		
		53. Falkirk	No overall control		
		54. Fife	No overall control		
		55. Highland	No overall control		
		56. Inverclyde	No overall control		
		57. Moray	No overall control		
		58. North Lanarkshire	Labour		
		59. Orkney	Independent		
		60. Perth & Kinross	No overall control		
		61. Renfrewshire	Labour		
		62. Scottish Borders	No overall control		
		63. Shetland Islands	Independent		
		64. South Lanarkshire	Labour		
		65. Stirling	No overall control		
		66. West Dunbartonshire	Labour	8	
	Northern Ireland				
	11 'Super' councils[a]	67. Lisburn & Castle City Council	No overall control		

17

	Committee	Party control	Executive	(Hybrid)
	68. Ards & North Down BC	No overall control		
	69. Mid & East Antrim BC	No overall control		
	70. Fermanagh & Omagh DC	No overall control		
	71. Antrim & Newtownabbey BC	No overall control		
	72. Mid Ulster DC	No overall control		
	73. Armagh City Banbridge & Craigaron BC	No overall control		
	74. Causeway Coast & Glens BC	No overall control		
	75. Belfast City Council	No overall control		
	76. Newry, Mourne & Down DC	No overall control		
	77. Derry City & Strabane DC	No overall control		
Total 415			338	(4)

Notes: [a] Since May 2014; [b] Since May 2012; [c] Since May 2013; [d] Alternative arrangements since 2001; [e] The Local Government (Scotland) Act 1973 allows local authorities to devolve most decision-making to a committee, sub-committee or officer of the council, which they have tended to do until recently; [f] Since May 2015; [g] Since April 2015.
Source: Council websites, BBC, House of Commons Library

18

No councillors should be paid more than the median gross weekly full-time earnings in their locality

Since the Paris Commune, working-class organisations have demanded that elected representatives be paid no more than the people they are representing. In Croydon in 2014/15, according to the council's website and neighbourhood statistics, 15 councillors received more than £571 per week (the median gross weekly full-time earnings in the locality). Conversely, in Labour Hartlepool (a unitary authority responsible for all services, where in 2012/13 directly elected mayor Stuart Drummond had received £63,902, or 11 times the basic allowance of backbench councillors) no councillor, after a change to the committee system in 2013/14, received more than £494 per week (the median gross weekly full-time earnings in the locality). The above analysis suggests that the prospect of fewer and lower levels of SRAs may be the main reason why only 13 councils have reverted to the committee system since the Localism Act.

Standards and codes of conduct

New Labour's Local Government Act 2000, although it established a Standards Board for England, also introduced executive government. This undoubtedly increased the potential for serious corruption because of the concentration of decision-making powers in fewer hands, with cabinets appointed by leaders and directly elected mayors (see Chapter Two). For example, Lord Hanningfield was Tory Leader of Essex County Council from 2001 until his resignation in 2010. In the House of Lords he served as an opposition whip and a Shadow Minister for education and transport. On 5 February 2010 it was announced that Hanningfield would be charged with offences under section 17 of the Theft Act 1968 relating to false accounting for claims for overnight accommodation. Hanningfield had claimed £99,970 in 'overnight subsistence' over the previous seven years despite living only 46 miles from Westminster, in West Hanningfield, and having a full-time chauffeur provided by the local authority at the taxpayers' expense (*Daily Telegraph*, 2 July 2009). On 26 May 2011 Hanningfield was found guilty. Moreover, on 26 September 2012, under the Proceeds of Crime Act 2002, he was ordered to pay back £37,000. Meanwhile Essex County Council was still waiting for £50,000 that it was owed by Hanningfield related to spending on its credit cards. The disgraced peer racked up a £287,000 bill between 2005 and 2010 (*Essex Chronicle*, 13 June 2013).

The Localism Bill 'originally entirely removed the requirement for local councils to maintain a code of conduct, intending to make it a voluntary matter' (House of Commons Library, 2016e, p 4), although the government changed course during the last weeks of the passage of the Bill, when peers in the House of Lords successfully promoted a number of amendments supporting a standards system in local government. Hence, although the Localism Act abolished the Standards Board (following the amendments in the House of Lords) councils do have to adopt a code regarding the conduct that is expected of members and co-opted members of the authority when they are acting in that capacity, rather than creation of a code being a voluntary matter. The code must be consistent with the Nolan principles of public life, that is, selflessness, integrity, objectivity, accountability, openness, honesty and leadership; and the monitoring officer must establish and maintain a register of interests of members and co-opted members of the authority.

Open Public Services

The Tory-led Coalition government's delayed White Paper on *Open Public Services* was published in July 2011. Commentators have been divided on its significance. For example, according to the late left Labour MP Michael Meacher's blog, the White Paper was 'just the softening up to the real meat which is indiscriminate privatisation across the whole range of public services'. Conversely, in press releases dated 11 and 12 July 2011 Alan Downey, head of KPMG's Public Sector Business, stated:

> The White Paper marks a watershed in the approach to the delivery of public services and could usher in a revolution that will transform the public sector landscape … What the Government needs to do next is … to move quickly to translate its statement of intent into practice … publishing a comprehensive list of the services that are to be opened up to competition and the timetable for allowing potential new providers to bid.

The White Paper's privatisation model was taken directly from a report called *Payment for Success*, published in 2010 by three senior partners at KPMG (Downey et al, 2010). In February 2011 David Cameron appointed Paul Kirby, one of the authors, as the government's head of policy development. Kirby has now returned to KMPG. In the KPMG model (Downey et al, 2010, pp 9–12) there are three types of publicly funded provision:

1. 'personal services' (for example, education and health), which should 'replicate the way that … real consumer markets work');
2. 'national services – where central government should be a strong national customer, but not necessarily the provider' (for example, courts, prisons, probation, immigration, national roads, benefits and job centres);
3. 'local community services' (for example, council environmental, leisure, children's, housing and economic development services), where there should also be 'a structural separation of provider from purchaser' plus the handing back of some services 'to the community' (for example, libraries that 'are spending scarce resources on premises').

The *Open Public Services* White Paper also divided the privatisation menu for public services into these three categories (HM Government, 2011, p 12).

One of the other key themes of the White Paper was local democracy: 'Both elected and unelected consumer and citizen champions will need to take a prominent role in pushing for increased quality and greater choice' (HM Government, 2011, p 15). For example, as George Jones noted, 'democratically-elected representatives will hold providers to account through the process of local overview and scrutiny, and increasingly will commission services from a wide range of providers to ensure that the voters have the choice they want'. But, what George Jones (2010) also refers to as the 'sub-localism' of 'unelected consumer ... champions' will further undermine the position of elected councillors. 'People, according to the White Paper, should also "use their voice in designing and managing the services they use..." (HM Government, 2011, p 11). However, this can mean no more than making your own cuts. For example, around 100 councils are currently offering budget consultations on which services to cut as part of the "big society" in action' (Latham, 2011a, p 396).

The White Paper also claimed that public employees would be empowered through the formation of mutuals: 'We are giving public sector staff new rights to form new mutuals and bid to take over the services they deliver, empowering millions of public sector staff to become their own bosses' (HM Government, 2011, pp 42–3). Yet, as Steve Davies, in his report *Mutual Benefit?* written for Unison concluded, the fact that the Tory-led Coalition government had

> nothing to say about the extension of mutualism in the private sector in general, or among the private sector contractors providing public services in particular, shows the hollowness of the government's claims and the lack of commitment to the values of mutualism. The real objective is to shrink the state and marketise all public service provision. The government is not interested in whether public service mutuals will exist in five years' time, just so long as they form a useful vehicle for the break-up of the public sector today. (Davies, S., 2011, p 31)

Publication of the first update of the White Paper, scheduled for November 2011, was delayed until March 2012. Central to it were the proposals for statutory choice frameworks in personal care and support; early education; schools; higher education; further education and skills; NHS primary care (GPs); NHS secondary care; social housing; and commissioned services (courts, prisons, offender management, driver and vehicle licensing, police IT and training, infrastructure and back-office functions); and choice champions (HM Government, 2012). But the key contradiction at the heart of the first updated White Paper, as David Walker pointed out, was that: 'Urging people to ask for more, to demand redress, to insist on their rights (which may even be legislated for) sits uneasily alongside austerity and cuts that have barely begun to bite' (*Guardian Professional*, 12 April 2012).

The second White Paper update, on 16 May 2013, claimed that the Open Public Services programme was 'releasing the grip of state control and putting power into people's hands'. Statutory choice frameworks and choice champions had been the main proposals in the first update; hence, as the second update noted, a call for evidence was launched on 12 February 2012 (which ran for 12 weeks and closed on 11 May 2012) regarding the possibility of introducing legislation that would 'enshrine user choice in a single piece of legislation'. The government engaged 172 stakeholders online and at stakeholder round-table events, and received 'a mixed response'. Therefore, the government decided not to proceed with 'a legislated right', but instead published its Choice Charter on 16 May 2013, which provides 'a framework within which all public services operate'. Yet there could be no real choice in public services when they were being cut on such a draconian scale. The Tory-led Coalition government's emphasis on user rights and choice was therefore vacuous rhetoric.

Seconding 'experts' into Whitehall departments to develop policy represented the effective privatisation of policy making. Nor are outsourced public services transparent and democratically accountable, as they are not covered by freedom of information legislation, and 'commercial confidentiality' is frequently cited as an excuse not to divulge information on their performance. Thus, as Zoe Williams states, 'a "shadow state" is emerging, where a small number of companies have large and complex stakes in public service markets, and a great deal of control over how they work' (2012, p 4).

Outsourcing

Under the Tory-led Coalition government, according to Information Services Group consultancy, the number of outsourced contracts rose by 125%, from 526 under the last Labour government to 1,185. The UK outsourcing market is now the second-largest in the world outside the US; and the amount spent on outsourced public services almost doubled from £64 billion under New Labour to £120 billion under the Coalition government. Broken down by sector, the value of central government contracts rose sharply, from £37 billion under New Labour to £67 billion. In healthcare, it grew from £9 billion to £16.5 billion; in education from £1.8 billion to £3.7 billion; and in local authorities from £16 billion to £32.5 billion. Separate research by OC&C Strategy Consultants (who forecast that £1 in every £3 spent by government and local authorities on delivering public services will go to outsourcing companies) suggested that outsourcing rose by one third in the 2010–15 Parliament (*Financial Times*, 30 April 2015).

Public Private Partnerships (PPPs) are used to fund major capital investments. They cover a range of business structures and partnership arrangements, including joint ventures, the sale of equity stakes in state-owned businesses and outsourcing where private sector operators use existing public sector assets, as well as the Private Finance Initiative (PFI), discussed below. PPP contracts usually last 10 years, with an option for a further five years.

The European Services Strategy Unit's database of PPPs for ICT and corporate services, planning and regulatory services, educational support services, police support services, fire and rescue support services, property services, highway services and waste and environmental services at the end of 2013 is titled *UK Outsourcing Expands Despite High Failure Rates*. The 45 waste management contracts included are virtually all PFI projects, valued at £29.8 billion, of which nine include household waste collection and other local environmental services. The total value of the 60 contracts was £13,442 million and they employed 26,575 workers. Three companies – Capita, BT and Mouchel – had a 58.9% market share of operational contracts by contract value and 63.2% share of staff employed. Just over 38% of the contracts by value and 38.4% of jobs were in the North. In 2011 the North had a 50% share of contracts, and the shift southwards illustrates significant increases in the value of contracts in the West Midlands, London and the South East/South. London, the South East/South and South West had 45% of contracts, 35.4% by value and 34.2% of jobs. The equivalent figures in 2007 were nearly half this level, at 24.2%, 21.2% and 19.3% respectively. Conversely, there were only one PPP contract in Wales, worth £100 million and employing 110 people; two in Scotland, worth £415 million and employing 380 people; and none in Northern Ireland. The level of contract terminations and problems has remained at the high level of over 22% (see Whitfield, 2014).

The PFI model was first launched in 1992 as part of the then Conservative government's initiative to increase the level of private sector involvement in the delivery of public services. PFI contracts are usually for 25–30 years. In recent years the cost of PFI – due in part to the economic downturn – has risen dramatically. Consequently, it is currently very difficult for PFIs and PPPs to demonstrate value for money as compared with conventional public sector projects, where governments build or purchase physical assets and use public sector employees or a private contractor to deliver the required service. The PF2 model was launched on 5 December 2012, but, unlike PFI, it requires construction companies to invest a substantial amount of their own money as equity, which acts as a buffer against the risk borne by lenders. This allows investments still to happen while deferring their budgetary impact to the future, when future taxpayers must bear it. The effect, as Mark Hellowell concludes, is also likely to be an increase in the cost of private finance faced by public authorities because equity carries a higher rate of return than loans.[1]

Table 1.2 shows that in the UK on 31 March 2012 there were 717 PFI projects with a total capital value of £54.6 billion, which is normally calculated at the financial close of the project. By 31 March

2015 there were 723 projects (578 in England, 93 in Scotland, 29 in Northern Ireland and 23 in Wales), of which 679 were operational; and the total capital value had risen to £57.7 billion (HM Treasury, 2016a, p 5). Meanwhile, companies that had been awarded contracts to build and maintain state schools for 25 years had doubled their money by selling on PFI projects just four years after finishing them. Four contractors alone made profits of more than £300 million – Balfour Beatty, Carillion, Interserve and Kier (*Independent*, 4 June 2014). Moreover, more than 200 schools built in Scotland under PFI schemes are now at least partially owned by offshore investment funds.

Table 1.2: UK PFI portfolio, 31 March 2012

	England	Scotland	Northern Ireland	Wales	Total
Number of projects	569	85	39	24	717
Capital cost (£bn)	46.5	5.7	1.9	0.5	54.6
Total estimated PFI payments (£bn)	260.6	30.8	7.2	2.8	301.4
Total estimated future PFI payments (£bn)	208.5	25.3	6.1	2.0	241.9
% of current commitments paid to date	20	17.8	15.2	27.9	
Total estimated committed cost per head (£)	4,917	5,811	4,000	903	
Total estimated future cost per head (£)	3,933	4,815	3,444	653	

Source: HM Treasury

In one project in Edinburgh, 17 new schools were built, with the council paying £1.5 million a month. The Edinburgh schools were closed for repairs in 2016 after construction faults were found; 7,600 primary and secondary school children were affected by the closures (*BBC News Scotland*, 22 August 2016).

Social impact bond projects are the newest 'buy now, pay later', off-balance-sheet schemes to increase private financing of public services. Currently 54 are operational in 13 countries, with at least a further 23 at the planning or procurement stage. The UK is the global leader, with 32 operational projects with outcome payments valued at £91 million, followed by the US with nine projects (Whitfield, 2015, p i). Moreover, as Whitfield (2015, p ii) notes,

> Payment-by-Results is a fundamental part of social impact bond projects and the UK's Troubled Families contracts achieved 100% performance even in major industrial cities and assumed the turnaround in people's lives was permanent!

A poll conducted for campaign group We Own It in November 2015 showed that:

- 61% of the population think that local and central government should run services in-house as the default;
- only 21% want to see more outsourcing;
- 67% of people think public service contracts and performance data should be publicly available;
- only 22% think Atos, Capita, G4S and Serco are motivated by providing the best service to the public, which 80% think should be important.

The above findings are hardly surprising in the light of recent scandals over outsourced services. In 2013 the Serious Fraud Office launched a criminal investigation into G4S and Serco, both large outsourcing companies, over allegations that they had overcharged on government contracts to provide electronic tagging of prisoners. In September 2015 G4S lost the contract for running a young offenders' facility, following its assessment as inadequate amid concern over the degrading treatment of detainees. At the end of 2015 the government was found to be paying Serco £1 million to run an empty secure children's unit for seven weeks. Moreover, a comprehensive review by the New Economics Foundation concluded that there is no empirical evidence that the private sector is more efficient (TUC and NEF, 2015).

Although outsourcing might mean cheaper services in the short term, there is a knock-on effect on morale and the quality of service provided and, in the longer term, flexibility and control are lost. For example, a report on the impact of outsourcing back-office functions at West Sussex County Council (WSCC) to Capita found that the outsourcing deal had led to lower-quality services, lower staff morale and less transparency and accountability. The contract in question is worth £154 million over 10 years and was signed in June 2012. The functions outsourced through the contract – known as the Services Outsourcing Contract – included everything from recruitment, human resources management and payroll to customer service centres and online service delivery. The key findings were as follows:

- 50% of respondents felt that services had got worse and just 2% said they had improved;
- 65% of staff felt they weren't offering a better service under Capita, and 55% felt more under pressure;
- the contract was preventing innovation and leading to a standardised treatment of service users;
- 70% of respondents disagreed or strongly disagreed with the statement 'There is good morale in my workplace';
- 76% of staff transferred from WSCC felt that morale was lower since transferring to Capita (Holt, 2015).

Between January 2012 and October 2013, Conservative Barnet Council outsourced its care for people with disabilities, legal services, cemeteries and crematoria, IT, finance, HR, planning and regeneration, trading standards and licensing, management of council housing, environmental health, procurement, parking and the highways department. On 15 December 2014 – by a majority of one – a full council meeting voted for cuts and 'alternative delivery models' for another tranche of services, including libraries, rubbish collection and children's speech therapy. Hence, as Aditya Chakraborty noted:

> For those who live and work in Barnet, their local affairs
> are now handled remotely by people hundreds of miles
> away, who know nothing about them or the area. Payroll
> for what remains of council staff is done in Belfast, while
> for schools it's Carlisle. Pension queries go to Darlington.
> Benefits end up in Blackburn. Parking notices come from
> Croydon. Calls to the local library are first directed to
> Coventry. Even births, deaths and marriages are managed
> in Brent. (*Guardian*, 16 December 2014)

Hence, as Chakraborty concluded: 'if you want to see what the
next five years of cuts hold for your local services – whether David
Cameron or Ed Miliband get in will make little odds for town halls
– you'd best pay close attention to what Barnet is doing' (*Guardian*,
16 December 2014).

Furthermore, Barnet aims to reduce its directly employed staff by
90%, from 3,200 in September 2012 to 322 by 2020; and website
copies of its two contracts with Capita state that it is 'legally obliged
to redact information that Capita has designated as confidential and
commercially prejudicial'. Similarly, the London Borough of Bromley
– despite having £130 million in reserves, unlike Barnet, which has
none – aims to contract out most of its services to private companies,
reducing the number of council employees from 4,000 to 300. And
Tory Northamptonshire County Council aims to outsource all services
and make cuts of £68 million. It will move away from delivering
services directly, by 4,000 staff, to a 'Next Generation Model' whereby
an 'expert core' of only 150 directly employed staff will commission
them instead.

There has always been a flow of single-service local government
contracts that have returned to in-house provision because they have
been terminated either due to poor performance or at the completion
of the contract. For example, since 2012 Islington Borough Council
has brought housing management, gas servicing and housing repairs
in-house. But such developments 'do not represent a "wave" of re-
municipalisation or re-nationalisation in the UK when compared

with the increasing rate of outsourcing and privatisation' (Whitfield, 2014, p 9). For, as the arvato UK Quarterly Outsourcing Index shows, contracts worth £2.08 billion were signed across the UK public and private sectors between January and March 2016, a sharp rise from the £414 million agreed in the final quarter of 2015. Overall, 65% of spend came from the public sector and 35% from businesses. Local government clients signed double the number of deals in the first quarter of 2016 compared to the same period in 2015, with a contract value worth £348.6 million.

Furthermore, the continuation of austerity policies, with further large cuts in public spending planned up to 2020, will increase budget pressures on local authorities and other public bodies to obtain 'savings' (see Chapter Four). The severing of public sector employment responsibilities means less concern for the terms and conditions of employment. Staff are increasingly transferred between employers, with drastic consequences for the continuity of terms and conditions, pensions, training and career development for most staff. In-house service reviews and improvement plans are replaced by options appraisals, business cases and procurement, frequently carried out by management consultants. CAs (see Chapter Two) will also have an increasing role in setting infrastructure and service priorities.

Moreover, shared services projects or joint service delivery between public bodies are likely to increase. For example, the Local Government Association's (LGA) website shows that in October 2015 at least 337 councils across England were engaged in 416 shared service arrangements resulting in £462 million of efficiency savings. The biggest partnerships saved up to £2.5 million per year, although more than half of all partnerships saved less than £100,000. Back-office functions, such as legal, audit and human resources are the most common shared services, which offer the smallest savings. The biggest savings were made in sharing procurement and capital assets (House of Commons Library, 2016f, p 9). Some Local Authority Trading Companies have been closed down after failing to make profits. For example:

- Bournemouth Borough Council's Bank of Bournemouth, set up in 2014, was forced to close in 2015 after lending to just over 22 businesses in 18 months (*Bournemouth Echo*, 8 December 2015).
- Shropshire Council's Inspiring Partnerships and Enterprises was forced to close in 2016 after securing 'minimal external business' and suffering from huge overheads (*Local Government Chronicle*, 19 February 2016).
- Kent County Council pulled the plug on a string of trading companies at a loss of £191,000; and a member of staff was sacked after auditors found funds had been misappropriated (*Kent OnLine*, 23 August 2016).

If the alternative economic and political strategy proposed in Chapter Five were to be implemented, such 'savings' would not be needed. Meanwhile:

- private providers should be subject to freedom of information requests;
- public service contracts, performance and financial data should be publicly available;
- before any outsourcing of services or privatisation of assets takes place there should be public consultation;
- the public should have the right to recall providers who do a bad job;
- there should always be an in-house bid on the table (or a reason given if there isn't), with social value the priority (We Own It).

The neoliberal transformation of cities and councils

Why 79 local government representatives attended the international property market's biggest trade event in March 2015

Le marché international des professionnels de l'immobilier (MIPIM) is an international property event hosted in Cannes annually over a period of four days.[2] The event was attended by 79 local government representatives – funded by private sector developers – from the following 24 councils:

- the City of London (11)
- Coventry (7)
- Ealing and Leicester (6 each)
- Haringey, Hounslow and Birmingham (4 each)
- Warwickshire, Solihull, Northamptonshire, Manchester, Barking & Dagenham and Croydon (3 each)
- York, Wakefield, Sheffield, Oldham, Newham, Leeds, Broxbourne and Bradford (2 each)
- Wandsworth, Newcastle and Harlow (1 each).

The majority of these councils – 18 out of 24 (75%) – are Labour controlled. The decades from Thatcher onwards, as the following examples show, have seen the neoliberal transformation of cities and councils, which now see the local state's key role as one of capital accumulation based on city centre development by property developers and big business.

Manchester

In 2004, according to the Office for National Statistics (ONS), Manchester was among the top five cities in Britain for worklessness, together with perennially blighted places such as Liverpool and Glasgow. By 2012 it had dropped out of the top five, while Birmingham entered the list for the first time in its history. In the period July 2014 to June 2015, when unemployment rate was 5.7% in the UK as a whole, 6.6% in London and 6.4% in Croydon, it was 8.1% in Manchester, 9.4% in Glasgow, 10% in Birmingham and 10.2% in Liverpool (ONS, 2015b).

There are two main criticisms of the Manchester model, however. The first is that regeneration has not benefited the whole population of the city equally. For, as the authors of the *Manchester Independent Economic Review* published in 2009 found, in the first decade of the new millennium, while in absolute terms every part of the city improved, inequality in the city had actually sharply increased. The richest bits of the city got richer at a much faster pace than the poorest bits. Hence Manchester's growing inequality, like London's, is proof that it has managed to create well-paying jobs for only a minority of its population. The second criticism links to that, and is made eloquently by Owen Hatherley, a Marxist architectural critic, who argues, in effect, that Manchester has lost its soul – it has swapped pop music for property redevelopment (Hatherley, 2010). The Haçienda, a famous Manchester nightclub, has been replaced by a block of luxury flats; and the city's council is often too obsessed with big, glitzy corporate projects and foreign direct investment, to the detriment of the city's organic growth.

Homelessness in Manchester has also increased by 150% in recent years. And the council has been pursuing legal action against a homeless group after they established a 'tent village' in the city centre. During the 2015 Tory party conference, as David Cameron was making his keynote speech about new 'affordable' homes for first-time buyers, the group occupied a Grade II listed building near the conference venue. Then, after being evicted, they occupied the historic Manchester Stock Exchange. The latter building is now owned by the former Manchester United players Gary Neville and Ryan Giggs, who allowed the squatters to use it as a hostel to house people during the winter. Their only stipulation was that surveyors and other workers should be able to gain access when needed to the building, which was being converted into a boutique hotel complete with basement gym, spa and rooftop private members' terrace (*Guardian*, 19 October 2015).

Birmingham

In February 2015, the city's Labour council announced that the city centre redevelopment project, Snow Hill, would provide additional new office space equivalent to 28 football pitches. And at MIPIM's March 2015 event the council offered for sale an even bigger development, the £1 billion Southern Gateway. Promotion of these prestige developments continues to be supported by funding diverted from front-line service budgets. Children's social services in Birmingham have been failed repeatedly by Ofsted, partly because of years of underfunding, and have now been taken over by a government Commissioner. The council borrowed most of the £188 million building and set-up costs for the new Library of Birmingham, which costs some £10 million a year to run. The result is that, only 18 months after it opened, 100 staff – around 50% – lost their jobs and opening hours were cut from 73 hours a week to just 40, while community libraries in the city are being closed or having their hours reduced.

The claims of job creation that these two projects make are likely to be grossly inflated. The Greater Birmingham and Black Country Local Enterprise Partnerships were launched in 2012 and have together generated 3,200 jobs. This, as Richard Hatcher shows, is a paltry increase of 0.25% in the 1.3 million jobs in the two areas – one new job for every 400 existing jobs. Moreover, many of these jobs require qualifications that put them beyond the reach of the majority of the unemployed. The unspoken hole in the centre of recent government and council job-creation schemes like these – their fatal flaw – is the reluctance of the private sector to invest in production. The reason for this is simple: it isn't profitable enough, and certainly much less profitable than investment in city centre property and knowledge-intensive business services.

The current principal policy instrument of Labour-controlled Birmingham City Council – the largest council in Britain – is the City Centre Enterprise Zone, which comprises 26 sites in the city centre. It is run by a public-private local enterprise partnership with a budget of £275 million to attract business investment by offering discounted business rates of up to £275,000 and easier planning rules for property development. It also enables borrowing against the anticipated rise in business rates in order to spend more immediately on infrastructure. 'In short, under the rules of the game imposed by the government, the council is cutting services and transferring the money to subsidise business profit' (Hatcher, 2015a, p 2).

In September 2014 Sir Bob (now Lord) Kerslake, former Permanent Secretary at the DCLG, was despatched to Birmingham as Eric Pickles' enforcer to carry out a review of the city's governance. The review was published in December 2014 and its most radical recommendation was a new vehicle for business intervention in the city's governance – an 'independent Birmingham leadership group' – which, as Richard Hatcher concludes, would 'subordinate the elected city council to the veto of a business oligarchy' (Hatcher, 2015a, p 4). In September 2015 Greg Clark (then Local Government Secretary and now Secretary of State for Business, Energy and Industrial Strategy) told a House of Commons inquiry that Birmingham's leadership had been too slow to make improvements to the council – putting the historic CA deal at risk. Clark also suggested that the government would consider taking over the council, as had happened in Tower Hamlets, if it failed to improve. Then, in October 2015, Sir Albert Bore, leader of the council, announced that he was stepping down from his post amid growing pressure for him to quit.

Croydon

Croydon Labour leader Tony Newman, Croydon North Labour MP Steve Reed and Croydon Central Tory MP Gavin Barwell (who is now Minister for Housing and Planning and for London) all uncritically endorsed the neoliberal consensus in October 2014 when the council unveiled its blueprint for devolved powers to deliver more than £5 billion of private sector regeneration (Latham, 2014). And there was little public debate about what would happen if Westfield and Hammerson failed to deliver on their £1 billion new shopping centre. Yet, as Sean Creighton, convenor of Croydon TUC's working party on the council's Growth Plan and its Croydon Assembly local economy working group, stated on the final day of the compulsory purchase order (CPO) inquiry:

> Bankruptcy ... is the big risk facing all developers and Westfield and Hammerson is not necessarily immune from

that possibility. The danger is that if Westfield/Hammerson demolishes the Whitgift Centre and does not proceed with construction, it will leave a derelict site, further blighting the town centre. If their scheme is not approved, then the existing shops have a chance to survive ... the partnership should be required to guarantee it would not demolish the existing centre until it had the finance and construction contract in place ... [and there could be] ... predatory buying out of either one or both of the companies ... creating further delays and possible abandonment of the project by new owners. (Quoted in *Croydon Advertiser*, 13 March 2015)

Following his report to Croydon TUC's annual general meeting on 12 March 2015, which unanimously agreed that the Westfield/Hammerson Partnership (CLP) should use only construction firms that employ their own workers, not umbrella companies, and pay at least the London Living Wage, on 13 March 2015 Creighton also asked the Planning Inspector to consider recommending that the Secretary of State modify the CPO to require CLP to implement the TUC's proposals: this was ignored. On the other hand, when Julie Belvoir, Director of Democratic and Legal Services for Croydon Council, requested that councillors refrain from commenting on the CPO inquiry – as Susan Oliver in her final submission to the Whitgift Centre CPO Inquiry on the 13 March 2015 noted – all of Croydon's 70 councillors agreed to say nothing, and none of them even complained about this request.

The 'new model of local government' in Croydon also includes:

- The *Croydon Council Urban Regeneration Vehicle* (CCURV). This is a partnership with John Laing – a major construction company and one of the founding members of the Consulting Association, which blacklisted building workers (House of Commons, 2013a, p 7). CCURV, according to the council, was established in November 2008; and the partnership is 'a 28-year exclusive joint venture … into which the Council commits land and in return John Laing invests equity funds as well as development expertise'.

- The *Croydon Strategic Metropolitan Board* (CSMB), a previously secret organisation that the *Croydon Advertiser* showed was established in May 2014 to oversee multi-million pound developments, including the Westfield and Hammerson scheme. Gavin Barwell MP was involved in the meetings before the group was formally created and named. He told the *Croydon Advertiser* there were "regular diarised meetings" involving the Croydon Partnership, the name given to Westfield and Hammerson's joint plan, Transport for London, the Mayor's Office and the council. At that point the meetings were chaired by politicians such as the former council leader Mike Fisher, or Sir Edward Lister, the former Deputy Mayor of London, policy and planning. Gavin Barwell further said: "I don't think the meetings should be formally minuted." Hence, as the *Croydon Advertiser* (17 February 2015) concluded: 'There is no public record of CSMB meetings or who senior council officers and elected members have met, nor any formal indication of how these meetings have shaped public policy. At no point has any politician, Labour or Conservative, admitted in the council chambers that a policy they were about to vote through had begun life as the concern of a private company. In short there is currently very little opportunity to scrutinise the political influence of big businesses in Croydon.' Subsequently, Croydon Council rejected the paper's request under the Freedom of Information Act for the minutes of the CSMB's six meetings held since May 2014 'on the grounds that this would prejudice both the "effective conduct of public affairs" and the commercial interests of the private companies involved, to whom it has promised the discussion will "remain confidential"' (quoted in the *Croydon Advertiser*, 17 April 2015).

- The *Develop Croydon Forum* (DFC) was formed in 2012 'to provide a collaborative, private sector-led approach to promoting the London Borough of Croydon and encouraging inward investment. It currently represents up to 50 key stakeholders, across the private, public and third sectors, who want to realise the regeneration and economic renewal of the borough.' DFC 'also leads a Croydon delegation to the international property market's biggest trade event, MIPIM, in France'. And, at MIPIM's March 2015 conference, Croydon Council's executive director Jo Negrini told potential investors that the council was "using its powers to take the risk out of development" (quoted in the *Croydon Advertiser*, 20 March 2015). Meanwhile Croydon TUC – at the full meeting of Croydon Council on 9 October 2014 – had asked councillors to support the call by the charity War on Want, housing activists and trade unions not to attend MIPIM's first UK conference: but this request was rejected. Croydon Council was also represented at the second MIPIM conference, held at Olympia from 21 to 23 October 2015 – despite Croydon TUC at its meeting on 8 October 2015 again calling on Croydon councillors to say no to MIPIM. Moreover, securing devolutionary powers "to help fund Europe's largest regeneration project" was the major theme of DFC's conference held on 18 November 2015, when the full delegate rate was £420 including VAT (*Croydon News*, 24 August 2015).

In July 2015 Croydon Council loaned £3 million to Boxpark, the retailing centre built from discarded shipping containers next to East Croydon Station. But there are growing concerns among already established Croydon small businesses that the venture will enjoy a competitive advantage, having received a multi-million-pound subsidy from the Labour council, and that it will freeze out smaller Croydon artisan traders with its annual rents – expected to be set at around £14,000. This, of itself, is a massive financial leg-up for an in-coming business, and one which few existing Croydon small businesses either expect or receive. Indeed, according to *Inside Croydon*, 24 July 2015, the single Boxpark loan is £1 million more than has been distributed to existing small businesses and start-ups in the borough in the whole of the last seven years through a special development fund where the biggest loan allowed is £25,000.

Meanwhile Croydon Labour group's neoliberal approach is imploding. For example:

- George Osborne announced a yearly 1% reduction in social rents in his July 2015 budget to cut the housing benefit bill. Croydon Council's 30-year business plan had been drawn up in the expectation of a 1% annual rise in social rent income on top of inflation. Instead, it will now lose more than £3 million a year, leaving its budget £481 million below the £3.47 billion anticipated (*Croydon Guardian*, 16 October 2015).

- At the 2015 Tory party conference David Cameron announced that starter homes for sale to first-time buyers under 40 will replace 'affordable' homes for rent in planning deals with developers. Starter homes will be homes for sale at 80% of the market price, up to a value of £250,000 (£450,000 in London). They will be built by private developers and sold to first-time buyers. The Housing and Planning Act 2016 places a duty on local authorities to increase the supply of starter homes, with requirements that they are built as part of any large-scale development. This will mean diverting funding from existing affordable housing obligations (called Section 106 obligations). At present local authorities can oblige developers to build low-rent homes as part of any large scheme, as the price of planning permission. In future, this subsidy must be diverted to fund starter homes instead (Shelter, 2015, p 3). Moreover, Shelter's research – which assumes that by 2020 an average starter home may sell for £214,000 in England and £395,000 in London, both under the maximum price set by the government – also shows that to afford these prices at current average lending ratios in England an *income of £50,000* and a *deposit of £40,000* would be needed; and in London an *income of £77,000* and a *deposit of £98,000* would be needed. For a 95% mortgage on a starter home in England, an *income of £59,000* and a *deposit of almost £11,000* would be needed; and in London an *income of £97,000* and a *deposit of almost £20,000* would be needed.

- Grants from central government, which form the majority of Croydon's income, will be phased out by 2020 – when councils will also be able to keep 100% of local taxes and cut business rates under the Tories' latest devolution proposals. Hence, as Croydon

Council leader Tony Newman has warned, "less money coming to services" could leave the council "hopping around on one leg with our hands tied behind our back" (quoted in the *Croydon Guardian*, 7 October 2015).

- All the authority's 10,000-plus workforce – apart from school workers – have been offered voluntary redundancy in a bid to plug a £100 million funding hole from 2016 to 2019 in the budget. Staff have also been invited to permanently reduce their working hours or take early retirement. The council blames unexpected government cuts to funding for public health, adult learning and the care of asylum-seeking children for increasing the financial pressure already caused by dwindling local government budgets (*Croydon Guardian*, 13 November 2015).

- According to a report by the council, 215 families were at 'significant risk' of eviction in 2016 because they were unable to afford rents in Croydon, due to benefit cuts; and 90 families would be required to 'move to homes outside London and the South East' (quoted in *Croydon Advertiser*, 13 November 2015).

- Council leader Tony Newman warned that the EU referendum result could lead developers to cancel their projects in the town centre (*Croydon Advertiser*, 24 June 2016).

Hence, as Christian Wolmar argued when seeking selection as Labour's candidate for the 2016 London mayoral election, developers are not the answer to the capital's housing crisis, since developer-led schemes are "gutting … the capital's soul by forcing ordinary people out of the city through sky-high house prices and a lack of high-quality and genuinely affordable housing" (quoted in *Inside Croydon*, 1 July 2015). Moreover, the London Assembly Planning Committee found that some developers are deliberately paying too much for land to make providing affordable housing unviable, with several hiding behind confidential viability assessments (letter to Mayor of London Boris Johnson, 1 February 2016). This occurs all across Britain, according to the Committee's then chair, Nicky Gavron. But the problem is hitting Londoners the hardest, and here it is compounded by three factors.

> First, the ruling political class is compliant towards the super-rich and distanced not only from the housing conditions of the poor but also the middle classes, who now feel displaced by the global uber-wealthy. Second, the government's welfare cuts have been used to make prime neighbourhoods more attractive to rich foreign investors, as tenants and low-income households are priced out of spaces previously reserved for them by the state. Third, the unregulated private housing market disadvantages those who are already struggling to survive its excesses. (*Observer*, 24 January 2016)

According to Tim Roach, GMB Union General Secretary, Leeds City Council would need to build 100 new arenas and 100 new Trinity shopping centres to come anywhere near plugging the funding hole left by local government cuts (*Morning Star*, 7 October 2015). Hence, as is argued in Chapter Four, the council tax, stamp duty land tax and business rates should be abolished and replaced by a system of land value taxation plus a wealth tax and more progressive income tax to fund increased provision of directly provided public services, which will require the election of at least a social democratic government. As the geographer Martin Dodge insists, in London, Birmingham and Manchester:

> "At least in the 60s there was a strategic, grand vision. Now it's just raw capitalism and gangster development: if someone can develop a site they will." (Quoted in the *Guardian*, 6 June 2016).

Jeremy Corbyn was overwhelmingly elected as the Labour Party's leader with an anti-austerity manifesto in 2015. Therefore, to ensure that regeneration meets the needs of the majority – not the property developers and big business – popular campaigning is needed to consolidate summer 2015's left turn.

Notes

[1] http://blogs.lse.ac.uk/politicsandpolicy/the-move-from-pfi-to-pf2-is-likely-to-make-it-more-rather-than-less-expensive-to-deliver-new-healthcare-facilities-in-the-future/

[2] http://www.mipim.com/

2
IMPOSED 'METRO' MAYORS – NEW WINE IN OLD BOTTLES

The current legislation in Britain is modelled on that in the US, where in 2011 over 50 former US mayors were in prison for corruption (Latham, 2011a, p 99). This chapter therefore focuses on developments since the Localism Act 2011 that reinforce the main arguments against directly elected mayors (DEMs), and explains why the Tory government now wants combined authorities with imposed DEMs in English cities.

Greater London

New Labour's Greater London Authority Act 1999 created the Greater London Authority (GLA), which is a strategic regional authority with a DEM whose powers are as follows:

- Transport: control of the underground and London buses, taxis, Docklands Light Railway and most main roads (the London boroughs remain the highway and traffic authorities for 95% of roads);
- Economic development: attracting new investment;
- Environment: working with the boroughs on air quality, waste and so on;

- Planning: setting the overall strategic framework for the development of London (the boroughs continue to deal with local planning matters);
- Fire: the London Fire and Emergency Planning Authority is responsible for London's fire service;
- Culture: playing a leading part in developing London's tourism, culture and sport;
- Health: promoting the improvement of the health of Londoners.

New Labour's Greater London Authority Act 2007 gave the DEM new lead roles on housing and adult skills; a strengthened role over planning; and additional strategic powers in a wide range of policy areas including waste, culture, sport, health and climate change. In addition, the DEM was given discretion to appoint political representatives to the Transport for London Board, appoint the Chair of the Metropolitan Police Authority or assume the role of Chair and appoint two members of the London Fire and Emergency Planning Authority Board.

Sections 186–231 of the Tory-led Coalition government's Localism Act:

- devolved executive powers over housing investment from the Homes and Communities Agency to the GLA;
- abolished the London Development Agency and transferred its city-wide roles on regeneration and management of European funding to the GLA;
- gave new powers for the Mayor of London to create Mayoral Development Corporations to focus regeneration where it is needed most, in partnership with London boroughs;
- gave boroughs control over more of the major local planning decisions that affect their local communities;
- the Mayor would consider only the largest planning applications in future;
- abolished the Mayor's duty to prepare four-yearly reports on the state of the environment in Greater London;

- gave the London Assembly a new power to reject the Mayor's final strategies by a two-thirds majority.

The Police Reform and Social Responsibility Act 2011 also gave London's DEM the same powers as directly elected Police and Crime Commissioners (PCCs) outside the GLA in England and Wales.

Nevertheless, as London's four local government DEMs in Hackney, Lewisham, Newham and Tower Hamlets plus the other London boroughs are responsible for providing all other services, London's DEM, as Ken Livingstone noted, still "has quite limited powers" (quoted in the *Guardian*, 30 January 2012). London clearly needed a strategic authority following Margaret Thatcher's abolition of the Greater London Council: but DEMs are designed to reduce local democracy, which is why Livingstone originally opposed them, although he showed the potential to use his position to advance progressive policies. Moreover, although in theory the mayor's powers are limited and Assembly Members are meant to hold the mayor to account, they can only reject the mayor's budget if they have a two-thirds majority in favour of doing so. Conversely, in the House of Commons, only a simple majority of MPs is required to defeat the government. In practice, the system is therefore top-heavy and the mayor holds most of the cards.

Local authority DEMs in England

New Labour's Local Government Act 2000 imposed one of four options on councils in England and Wales:

- a directly elected mayor with a cabinet;
- a directly elected mayor and council manager;
- a cabinet with leader;
- 'Alternative Arrangements' for an enhanced or streamlined committee system, if they so wished, only for English districts in two-tier areas with populations under 85,000 and the 22 Welsh councils.

The Local Government and Public Involvement in Health Act 2007 gave council leaders virtually the same powers as DEMs.

Imposed DEM referendums

Schedule 2, section 9N of the Localism Act gives the Secretary of State power to 'require a specified local authority to hold a referendum on whether the authority should operate a mayor and cabinet executive'. On 5 December 2011 this power was used to force Birmingham, Bradford, Bristol, Coventry, Leeds, Liverpool, Manchester, Newcastle, Nottingham, Sheffield and Wakefield to hold DEM referendums on 3 May 2012. Yet, as George Jones noted in his blog, these cities had had

> the opportunity to hold referendums since 2001 but did not want them. They could have had one if a public petition from only 5% of the electorate had been in favour of a referendum, but none reached the threshold. Central government has forced an unwanted referendum only once before, in 2002 on Southwark, where the 'no' vote was 68.6%. (Jones, 2012)

Meanwhile Liverpool City Council's Labour leader, Joe Anderson, had been in talks with ministers since September 2011 for additional powers and resources. And on 7 February 2012 – at an extraordinary meeting when Labour councillors were given a free vote – Liverpool City Council, according to its website, voted to move straight to the election of a DEM on 3 May 2012 without a referendum.

Nine out of the 10 cities with imposed mayoral referendums rejected DEMs on 3 May 2012

The average turnout in the referendums, according to the councils' websites, was only 28.3% (ranging from 33.5% in Bradford to 23.8% in Nottingham), which was lower than the 30% average turnout in the 41 previous referendums. The second-lowest turnout (24.1%) was in

Bristol – which voted yes – and where, as in Nottingham, there were no local elections that year. The average percentage of the electorate voting yes in the 10 cities was 11.7 (ranging from 15.8% in Bradford to 10% in Coventry). Even in Bristol only 12.7% of the electorate voted yes; and in the subsequent DEM election, held on 15 November 2012, the number of voters who were denied any say in the second round was greater than George Ferguson's majority. This occurs because the supplementary vote system is used to elect DEMs, which allows voters to record their first and second choices on their ballot papers, although they are not required to make a second choice. The first-choice votes are then counted. If a candidate obtains more than 50%, he or she is elected. If not, all the candidates other than the top two are eliminated and the second choices on the ballot papers of those voting for the eliminated candidates are counted if they are for the two remaining candidates. In Bristol, according to the council's website, there were 89,152 valid first-choice votes: George Ferguson received 31,321 votes (35.1%) and Marvin Rees 25,896 (29.1%). Therefore, as no candidate received more than 50%, all the other candidates were then eliminated. In the second round, Ferguson received 6,032 second preference votes; and Rees 5,363. Ferguson's total vote was then 37,353 (54.4%) and that for Rees 31,259 (45.6%). Hence Ferguson's winning margin was 6,094 votes on the second count; and 73,797 (out of the 89,152 who only in voted in the first round and did not make a second choice) were disenfranchised.

DEMs lead to cronyism, patronage and corruption

According to Peter Keith Lucas, the introduction of executive government by New Labour

> has undoubtedly increased the potential for serious corruption … The concentration of decision-making powers in fewer hands finds its most extreme example in the directly elected mayor, responsible for all executive functions, except those, which [s]he chooses to delegate

to [her] his cabinet or to officers. (Quoted in Latham, 2011a, p 103)

For example, the reign of Doncaster's former New Labour DEM Martin Winter was mired in controversy after a series of police and independent inquiries into his conduct (Latham, 2011a, p 104). On 8 March 2009 Stoke-on-Trent's former DEM and ex-Militant supporter Mark Meredith – then the highest-paid DEM – was arrested on suspicion of corruption. Subsequently, on 8 July 2009 Staffordshire Police announced that ex-mayor Mark Meredith, Councillor Ibbs and millionaire businessman Mo Chaudry would not face criminal charges. However, in November 2009 correspondence between Mo Chaudry, senior politicians (including Mark Meredith) and officers (including the former Council Manager Steve Robinson, who by then was chief executive of Cheshire West and Chester Council) revealed that they had secretly agreed to shut the Dimensions Leisure Centre splash pool in January 2008. Mo Chaudry would have been paid about £100,000 a year to offer cut-price entry at his Waterworld facility for Dimensions swimmers after the splash pool had been closed by the council, and was also offered £50,000 to provide free children's swimming sessions (Latham, 2011a, p 116).

The then Communities Secretary, Eric Pickles, appointed PricewaterhouseCoopers (PWC) on 4 April 2014 to carry out a best value inspection of the London Borough of Tower Hamlets (LBTH). PWC's report was published on 4 November 2014 and found no evidence of fraud, although it concluded that LBTH had 'failed to comply with its best value duty' in relation to the way grants were awarded and property sold (PWC, 2014, p 14). Pickles then imposed three commissioners on LBTH to oversee the awarding of grants and property sales until 31 March 2017 (*Local Government Chronicle*, 4 November 2014). However, as PWC also noted, under DEM Lutfur Rahman LBTH achieved a wide range of awards and performance measures. For example:

- in 2013 65% of pupils in the borough achieved five or more GCSEs at grade A★-C, including English and mathematics. This compares favourably to the 2013 national average of 59% of pupils achieving five or more GCSEs or equivalent at grade A★-C, including English and mathematics GCSEs;
- the Tower Hamlets Dementia Partnership was awarded the National Local Government Chronicle Health and Social Care Award in 2014 for having improved the lives of people with dementia, including their carers;
- the borough received a national award in 2014 for the highest number of sustainable new-build housing units completed;
- the authority's school meals service was awarded in 2014 for being the best in Britain at the Lead Association for Catering in Education awards;
- the authority became an accredited London Living Wage employer in 2014 (PWC, 2014, p 45).

In addition, LBTH has brought back the education maintenance allowance; provided bursaries for its university students; resisted turning schools into academies; absorbed the cost of council tax benefit cuts; and bailed out 2,500 families placed at risk by the Tories' bedroom tax (*Morning Star*, 8 November 2014). Nevertheless it was still the case that – even without the imposition of unelected officials – power in LBTH was too concentrated, since Rahman had 'reserved to himself substantially all of the decision making powers which it is legally possible for an executive mayor to exercise'. Thus, in relation to 'large areas' of LBTH's activities, Rahman had had 'ultimate decision making power' (PWC, 2014, p 45).

On 23 April 2015, the Election Commissioner ruled that the election of LBTH's mayor must be re-run after he found Rahman guilty of corrupt and illegal practices and ordered him to pay £250,000 in immediate costs from a bill expected to reach £1 million. Rahman's election agent, Alibor Choudhary, was also banned as a councillor, with immediate effect. The returning officer was instructed to arrange a new DEM election and a by-election in the Stepney Ward. "I will now ask the Commissioners", said Eric Pickles, "whether further resources or powers are necessary to help them stamp out this culture of corruption in Tower Hamlets" (quoted in *Public Finance*, 23 April 2015). But, as the *Guardian* (27 April 2015) concluded,

> a quicker and simpler mechanism than a petition to the electoral court is clearly needed. It is very unsatisfactory that it should have taken a year to get the election voided. It is also worrying that there seems to have been no appetite on the part of the police to investigate the allegations which the judge had no difficulty in substantiating.

On 29 April 2015 Eric Pickles announced that he had appointed two new commissioners, including former Metropolitan Police assistant police commissioner Chris Allison, in addition to the three commissioners appointed in November 2014. Their powers over grants, contracts and electoral administration were increased to cover "the whole of the local authority, as the commissioners see fit" (quoted in the *Morning Star*, 30 April 2015). The following day, at a rally in Stepney, Rahman confirmed that he was "exploring the possibility" of challenging the Election Commissioner's ruling. He also endorsed a close associate, Rabina Khan, as a candidate for the DEM election on 11 June 2015. Andrew Murray, Unite's chief of staff, told the rally: "I am not speaking in a personal capacity, I am speaking on behalf of the union ... and I am sending a message of support from our general secretary, Len McCluskey. Unite is proud to associate ourselves with Lutfur Rahman." He called the judgment "an undemocratic assault on the people of Tower Hamlets" that was both "racist" and "Islamophobic". George Galloway MP sent a recorded message that described the decision as "an anti-democratic, anti-Islamic and racist coup". Christine Shawcroft of Labour's National Executive Committee, and a trustee of Rahman's legal defence fund, said: "The lack of a sound evidence base, the factual inaccuracies, the dangerous claims made about British Muslims and the powers given to the state to intervene in elections set a disturbing precedent." Ken Livingstone, the former Labour Mayor of London, said in another recorded message that the judgment was "politically motivated" (quoted in the *Guardian*, 1 May 2015). And the Metropolitan Police said on 1 May 2015 that they had identified new material, which they were now considering in connection with 47 of the allegations originally reported to them (*Guardian*, 2 May 2015).

Shawcroft was suspended from the Labour Party for publicly supporting Rahman, but was reinstated on 7 July 2015 (*Morning Star*, 8 July 2015). In addition, McCluskey subsequently distanced himself from Rahman in a letter to the *Guardian* (13 May 2015) in which he stated that:

> Certainly, Unite has worked closely with Mr Rahman in developing a community centre in Cable Street … and we applaud his stand against using contractors who blacklist trade unionists … I am also concerned at the democratic implications of a judge dismissing an elected mayor – laws allowing for such a procedure, against which there appears to be no appeal, should be changed … However, I … cannot give him support on issues which are matters for the court and in which Unite has no involvement. In the election to choose his successor, Unite will, of course be supporting the Labour candidate.

Labour's John Biggs won the re-run DEM election, held on 11 June 2015, when the turnout, according to LBTH's website, was 10% lower than in May 2014. His majority after the second count was 6,370. Labour now controls the council, following its candidate winning the re-run Stepney ward by-election. And on 29 October 2015 Greg Clark, then Communities Secretary, announced that the government's commissioners would no longer have the power to directly run the council, although he noted that four would remain to carry out some functions and oversee further improvements.

DEMs remove the working class from this layer of local democracy and replace them with a brigade of full-time career politicians

All the 17 DEMs are full-time career politicians (Table 2.1). The majority of DEMs (13) are Labour, with two independents and one each from the Conservatives and Liberal Democrats. Torbay's electors – who have the one Conservative DEM – voted in May 2016 to revert to the cabinet and leader system of governance from 2019 (*BBC News*, 8 May 2016). There are only four women DEMs, and only two black and minority ethnic (BME) DEMs. Sadiq Khan, the first Asian and Muslim DEM, was brought up in a council house and his father was a bus driver; the father of Marvin Rees, the first black DEM, arrived in this country 50 years ago from Jamaica to signs saying: 'No Irish, no blacks, no dogs' (*Guardian*, 23 May 2016). London's previous DEM, old Etonian Boris Johnson, received the mayoral salary of £143,911 in 2015, which Khan now receives; and in the three years prior to 2012 Johnson earned £1.3 million as a *Daily Telegraph* columnist and from other freelance work. Johnson also benefited significantly from George Osborne's decision to scrap the 50p top rate of income tax – a move he strongly lobbied for (*Guardian*, 5 April 2012). In May 2015 Johnson was elected as MP for Uxbridge and South Ruislip. Hence the process of selection and election has produced a cohort of DEMs who are predominantly from the middle strata of society, white, male and middle aged – as is shadow home secretary Andy Burnham, who is Labour's candidate for Greater Manchester's first imposed DEM election in 2017 (*Guardian*, 10 August 2016). On the other hand, Steve Rotheram (who defeated Joe Anderson, whose post as Liverpool's DEM is unaffected by the new city region DEM system), Labour's candidate in Liverpool City Region's DEM election in 2017, is a former bricklayer and Parliamentary Private Secretary to Jeremy Corbyn (*BBC News*, 10 August 2016).

Table 2.1: The 17 directly elected mayors in England, September 2016

Authority name, type and population[a]	Mayor	Party	DEM's remuneration/ special responsibility allowance (£ rounded)	Councillors' basic allowance (£ rounded)	Differential 2016/17
Greater London: Strategic; 8,173,941	Sadiq Khan[c]	Labour	143,911	55,161[b]	2.6 x greater
Bedford Unitary Borough: 159,200	Tim Douglas	Labour	83,997	10,425	7.1 x greater
Bristol: Unitary City; 432,500	Marvin Rees[c]	Labour	77,268	11,530	6.7 x greater
Copeland: District Council; 70,600	Mike Starkie	Independent	53,063	3,063	17.3 x greater
Doncaster: Metropolitan Borough; 302,400	Ros Jones	Labour	60,600	12,120	5 x greater
Hackney: London Borough; 246,300	Philip Glanville[d]	Labour	89,439	10,366	8.6 x greater
Leicester: Unitary City; 329,600	Sir Peter Soulsby	Labour	58,287	10,247	5.7 x greater
Lewisham: London Borough; 275,900	Sir Steve Bullock	Labour	87,534	9,812	8.9 x greater
Liverpool: Unitary City; 466,415	Joe Anderson[c]	Labour	79,500	10,077	8.9 x greater
Mansfield: District Council; 104,466	Kate Allsop	Independent	59,930	6,248	9.6 x greater
Middlesbrough: Unitary Borough; 134,400	Chistopher Budd	Labour	61,300	6,130	11 x greater
Newham: London Borough; 308,000	Sir Robin Wales	Labour	81,029	10,829	7.5 x greater
North Tyneside: Metropolitan Borough; 200,800	Norma Redfearn	Labour	71,493	9,759	7.3 x greater
Salford: Unitary City; 233,900	Paul Dennett[c]	Labour	69,690	10,080	6.9 x greater
Torbay: Unitary; 131,000	Gordon Oliver	Conservative	54,990	8,249	7.7 x greater
Tower Hamlets: London Borough; 254,100	John Biggs	Labour	75,816	10,166	7.5 x greater
Watford: District Council; 91,700	Dorothy Thornhill	LiberalDemocrats	65,738	7,209	9.1 x greater

Notes: [a]2011 Census; [b]London Assembly members; [c]Since May 2016; [d]Since a by-election in September 2016 (after he replaced Jules Pipe who is now Sadiq Khan's planning chief) when the turnout was 18.6%, which was well below the average turnout of 25.5% for DEM-only elections.
Source: Greater London Authority/council websites.

DEMs are the optimal internal management arrangement for privatised local government services

In 1999 Capita Group plc, in its evidence to the Joint Committee on the Draft Local Government (Organisation and Standards) Bill, supported 'the introduction of elected mayors or their equivalent for all tiers and size of councils' because it considered that it was 'easier to develop and negotiate effective leading edge ... partnerships ... where the council has a strong leader and effective Chief Executive and that it helped if the leader is able to commit the council and to have control over his/her group' (Latham, 2011a, pp 106–7).

DEMs create an arena focused on personalities, not politics

In the 2012 Greater London DEM election, as George Jones pointed out in his LSE blog, the electoral campaigning 'degenerated into a clash of personality ... not about the candidates' personal styles of leadership but about personal aspects of their private lives' and 'the politics of celebrity, not about competing programmes of principle and policy'. Hence Boris Johnson's programme of budget cuts, underinvestment, above-inflation fare increases and attacks on jobs and services since 2008 were not seriously scrutinised; and Ken Livingstone's principled opposition to the government's austerity measures was obscured, as were his progressive positions on many of the key strategic areas within the mayor's remit. Examples of the latter are Livingstone's policies to introduce a living rent as the first stage to proper rent controls, which the mayor does not have the power to introduce; cut fares by 7%; support a programme of retro-fitting all London's buildings to make them energy efficient; not allow contracts to be awarded to firms that impose cuts in wages and conditions; and reinstate the education maintenance allowance.[1] Johnson's biographer Sonia Purnell dubbed him 'the mayor who never was' (*Guardian*, 2 May 2016) because:

> There are many – including not a few within and around
> City Hall itself – who believe that Johnson vacated that

post in all but name long before he officially ceased to be mayor.... In the 12 months since he became an MP – in anticipation of being crowned the new Tory leader – the malaise worsened....Livingstone [was] ... once the ultimate Tory hate figure.... But many Tories, with heavy hearts, now conclude that he was a 'better mayor'.

Owen Jones (*Guardian*, 7 May 2016) noted that the Conservative Party candidate for London's DEM, Zac Goldsmith

waged a campaign soaked in racism, in one of the most ethnically diverse cities on Earth, shamelessly exploiting anti-Muslim prejudices in an effort to secure a shameful victory. Khan was a candidate who 'repeatedly legitimised those with extremist views', he [Goldsmith] wrote in the Mail. London was offered a campaign of fear, smear and bigotry ... Now senior Tories are condemning the campaign as 'poisonous' and as 'outrageous'. Too late. The damage is done. And by condemning any alleged antisemitism on the left, and staying silent about anti-Muslim prejudice on the right, they reveal they have no interest in fighting racism.

DEM referendums have not increased turnout and lack voter support

The average turnout in the 56 DEM referendums held between May 1998 and May 2015, including in Greater London, was 29.6%. Actual turnout ranged from 63.8% in Berwick-upon-Tweed in June 2001 to 9.8% in Ealing in December 2002. Turnout in the 18 successful referendums averaged 28.9%, and ranged from 60.1% in Tower Hamlets to 15.5% in Bedford. The average turnout in the 37 referendums that voted against DEMs was 29.8% (only 0.9% better than in the successful referendum). Although the 34.1% turnout in the Greater London mayoral referendum on 7 May 1998 was 4.5% higher than the average turnout for all the 56 mayoral referendums, it was still lower than:

- the 64% turnout in the European Communities Membership referendum on 5 June 1975;
- the 50.1% turnout in the Devolution in Wales referendum on 18 September 1997;
- the 60.2% turnout in the Devolution in Scotland referendum on 11 September 1997;
- the 81.1% turnout in the Northern Ireland Good Friday Agreement referendum on 22 May 1998;
- the 47.7% turnout in the North East regional assembly referendum on 4 November 2004;
- the 42.2% turnout in the national voting reform referendum on 5 May 2011;
- the 84.6% turnout in the Scottish referendum on 18 September 2014 (Electoral Commission, 2011, p 19);
- the 72.2% turnout in the EU Membership referendum on 23 June 2016 (Electoral Commission, news release, 24 June 2016).

Turnout is affected by the decision to conduct the referendum on the same day as other elections. Three referendums coincided with a general election: Berwick-upon-Tweed, when the turnout was 63.8%; the Isle of Wight, when the turnout was 62.4%; and Tower Hamlets, when the turnout was 60.1%. A further 16 referendums were held at the same time as local council elections and in these the average turnout was 29.8%, ranging from 36% in Great Yarmouth to 21% in Mansfield. By contrast, in the 35 referendum-only votes, the average turnout was 27.4% (ranging from 41.8% in West Devon to 9.8% in Ealing). And in Copeland, when the mayoral referendum coincided with the May 2014 European Parliament election, the turnout was 33.9%.

The method of voting is also a major influence on turnout. Thus, when voting was entirely by post – 15 cases, mainly in the early 2000s, when postal voting experiments were conducted – turnout averaged 31.3%, but when voting was by post and in-person attendance at polling stations the turnout fell to 21.7%. Seasonal factors also affect turnout. In seven referendums held in January, for example, the average turnout was 29.9%. However, in five of these cases the ballot was conducted entirely by post, which boosted the turnout to 36.4% in Harlow, 39.8% in Plymouth, 25.9% in Newham, 36.3% in Shepway and 41.8% in West Devon. However, in Southwark – where the referendum was ordered by the Secretary of State – the turnout was only 11.2%; and in Salford it was 18.1%. Hence, as Rallings et al note, 'There is a disjuncture here between the claims made by some national politicians about the value of extending mayoral government and the reception given to those ideas by local politicians and voters alike' (2014, p 7).

DEM elections have not increased turnout and lack voter support

In the high-profile London-wide DEM elections – always held at the same time as the London Assembly elections – the average turnout between 2000 and 2016 was 39.9% (34% in 2000, 37% in 2004, 45.3% in 2008, 38% in 2012 and 45.2% in 2016), which is similar to the turnout at London borough council elections (see House of Commons Library, 2016b, p 27). The average turnout between 2002 and 2015 in the 15 London local authority DEM elections – also now always held at the same time as the London borough council elections – was 38.1%, which is also similar to the turnout at London borough council elections. The turnout in all of the 58 local authority DEM elections held between May 2002 and May 2016 averaged 39.1% (ranging from 66% in Bedford in May 2015 to 18.5% in Mansfield in October 2002). Although in DEM-only elections the average turnout falls to 25.5%, it rises to 35.3% when combined with either a local or European election; and in 15 cases (five in May 2005, four in May 2010 and six in May 2015) when the DEM contest was concurrent with a general election the average turnout was 55%. There is no correlation between turnout and the number and type of candidates contesting the DEM election. The level of rejected ballots is higher compared with local elections held in the same place on the same day. Similar differences occur when mayoral and local elections are held simultaneously; and in every case the percentage participating in the DEM election is lower than that participating in the local council election. Hence, as Rallings et al conclude, 'low turnout in mayoral elections necessarily impacts upon the ability of the holder of that office to claim widespread local support' (2012, p 1).

DEMs have an undemocratic voting system

Out of the 58 local government DEM elections held between 2002 and 2016, in only 18 (less than a third) – Copeland (2015), Hackney (2010 and 2014), Middlesbrough (2002, 2007 and 2011), Newham (2002, 2010 and 2014), Watford (2006 and 2014), Tower Hamlets (2010), Leicester (2011 and 2015), Liverpool (2012 and 2016), North Tyneside (2013) and Lewisham (2014) – did the successful mayoral candidates get over 50% of the votes cast on the first count. Analysis of the results of the other 40 contests – where a second count was necessary – shows the absurdity of the SV system used to elect DEMs, since voters need to be able to guess which two candidates will be the leaders on the first count. Any voter who is unable to do so has no effect on the second round that actually decides the result. Moreover, in 35 (88%) of the 40 contests where there was a second count, the number of voters who were denied any say in the second round was greater than the eventual majority of the winning candidate. For example:

- Stoke-on-Trent in October 2002, where the winning margin was 314 votes on the second count and 18,922 voters were disenfranchised;
- Doncaster in June 2009, where the winning margin was 354 votes on the second count and 24,902 were disenfranchised;
- Mansfield in May 2011, where the winning margin was 67 votes on the second count and 3,735 were disenfranchised;
- Middlesbrough in May 2015, where the winning margin was 256 votes on the second count and 10,528 were disenfranchised;
- Bristol in May 2016, where the winning margin was 29,173 votes on the second count and 50,333 were disenfranchised.

A YouGov poll commissioned by the *Evening Standard* just over a week before the 2012 London DEM election found that only 47% of voters knew and understood the two-vote system; another 18% knew about the method but not how it worked; and 25% admitted that they did not know anything about SV. Hence Rallings et al conclude that because a two-round system with only two candidates in the second round or the first-past-the-post system would probably not increase turnout, we need to provide 'information about how the system works in practice' (2014, p 17). Their proposal excludes using the single transferable vote system (STV) for DEM elections. Yet STV has been used in local elections in Northern Ireland since 1973 and in Scotland since 2007. Nine New Zealand local authorities use the STV for both local and DEM elections (see Latham, 2011a, Appendix 12), although the contest for a single vacancy cannot be proportional, since when only one person can win office, by definition the winner takes all. However, STV ensures that the ultimate winner has majority support. As the political scientist Nigel Roberts explains,

> This means that they need to win second, third, and even fourth preference support from voters who don't initially vote for them. Candidates and voters who understand this … are more likely to be both effective and satisfied by the outcome of the election. (*Fairfax NZ News*, 20 September 2013)

Therefore, the fairest and most consistent solution would be to use the STV until DEMs are abolished. And STV should be used in all elections, with the age of adulthood, including the right to vote, set at 16 to reflect the other freedoms and responsibilities acquired by many young people at that age.

DEMs cannot be removed

DEMs can be removed only if there is evidence of corruption or other law breaking. Hence, as George Jones (2012) emphasises in his blog, 'if a DEM turns out bad or ineffective during the four-year term, there is no possibility for the removal of a DEM until the next election'. Therefore, Jones concludes, 'Advocates of community empowerment should give councils the right to a vote of no-confidence and enable the people to petition to submit the DEM to a new election.'

Combined authorities and imposed DEMs

The Democracy, Economic Development and Construction Act 2009 (passed by the New Labour government) set out clear roles and functions for the Regional Development Agencies, which were subsequently abolished by the Localism Act. However, Section 15 gives the Secretary of State power to transfer local public functions. The latter clause was 'inspired by the Core Cities Group', led by the leaders of Birmingham, Bristol, Leeds, Liverpool, Manchester, Newcastle, Nottingham and Sheffield councils, which described itself as aiming in partnership 'to enable each City to enhance their economic performance and make them better places to live, work, visit and do business' (quoted in Bentley, 2012, p 75).

By September 2015, 34 devolution proposals had been received from local areas in England (NAO, 2016, p 4). Now there are 10 CAs in England covering 16.1 million people: Cornwall, East Anglia, Greater Lincolnshire, Greater Manchester, Liverpool City Region, North East, Sheffield City Region, Tees Valley, West Midlands and West of England (NAO, 2016, p 43). The devolution deal for Cornwall, agreed with ministers on 6 July 2015, gives the county greater control of adult skills spending and regional investment. It also introduces an integrated health and care system, although Cornwall will not be required to elect a mayor. This was the first devolution deal agreed with a county authority. City CAs will still be required to have DEMs (*Public Finance*, 20 July 2016). Dick Cole, leader of Mebyon Kernow, the Party for Cornwall, a councillor but not part of Cornwall's ruling Independent–Liberal Democrat coalition, was unimpressed by the devolution deal because he wants a National Assembly similar to Scotland's and Wales's. As Richard Hatcher notes, the combined authority 'marks a fundamental change in the model of local government in England' (2015b, p 1). Moreover:

- before the 2015 General Election 47% of chief executives and leaders believed their authority would be part of a CA by 2020; and post-election this figure had increased to 58%;
- before the General Election only 12% of chief executives and leaders favoured DEMs; post-election this figure had risen to 22%; and the proportion who disagreed had fallen from 83% to 61% (PWC, 2015, p 13).

On 3 November 2014, the Tory-led Coalition government foisted a 'metro' DEM system on Greater Manchester without a referendum. A DEM had previously been rejected by Manchester City Council voters following the imposed May 2012 referendum. The DEM will not be answerable to a London-style directly elected assembly but to a cabinet comprising the 10 Greater Manchester council leaders, which must be consulted on the DEM's strategies. The DEM, not due to be in place until 2017, may be overruled if two-thirds of the council leaders disagree with a decision. The DEM will also have control of a £300 million housing investment fund and be responsible for strategic planning, including the power to create a statutory spatial framework for Greater Manchester, which will need to be approved by a unanimous vote of the DEM's cabinet. He or she will also have responsibility for a devolved transport budget, with a multi-year settlement to be agreed at the next spending review; and responsibility for franchised bus services, subject to consultation by Greater Manchester, and for integrated smart ticketing. The DEM will also take on the role of Police and Crime Commissioner. The Greater Manchester CA will take control of public service reform through apprenticeship grants, further education, some welfare funds and the integration of health and social care. Although much remains unresolved in the deal – for example, education is missing – it also devolves an extra £2 billion of spending to the mainly Labour leaders of the 10 boroughs (*Guardian*, 3 November 2014). Yet, as Will Hutton noted:

Greater Manchester may now be in control of £7 billion. But that would have been £10 billion four years ago – and it will be around £5 billion on current spending plans in 2018/19 as part of the drive to lower public spending to at least the same proportion of GDP it was in 1948. No advanced country has ever subjected its cities to such devastating expenditure cuts in modern times. (*Observer*, 9 November 2014)

In January 2015 Manchester People's Assembly and the Greater Manchester Association of Trades Union Councils (GMATUC) launched a petition to campaign for the right of people in Greater Manchester to have their say before the 'Devo Manc' deal is implemented (*Morning Star*, 10 January 2015).

In 2016 Greater Manchester became the first English region to get full control of its £6 billion health and social care budget – which, Andy Burnham warned, will create a 'two-tier' health service (*Manchester Evening News*, 25 February 2015). Burnham's warnings were brushed aside both by careerist Labour councillors and by many of his Manchester Labour MP colleagues, although Wigan Labour MP Lisa Nandy criticised the complete lack of a democratic base for the changes being imposed top-downwards on the 'city region'. "Ministers have confirmed to me that no thought has yet been given to public scrutiny or involvement," she said. In addition, as Nandy further added, the three-week consultation on the impact of the changes had only 12 responses – 10 of them from local authority leaders who had brokered the deal in the first place. Nandy's view, as noted above, is shared by the GMATUC, and both Unite and Unison in Manchester are opposed to a DEM, for fear that whoever takes office will resort to wholesale privatisation and cuts in business tax. The plan does not provide any new money; and it does not restore the £3 billion of cuts in social care since 2010.

The Memorandum of Understanding [MoU] openly admits that 'some of the areas described in the MoU go beyond the statutory powers of NHS England and CCGs [clinical commissioning groups], and are often commissioned nationally', and that 'there will need to be an agreement as to the precise scope and extent of the commissioning functions that can lawfully be delegated' (Association of Greater Manchester Authorities et al, 2015, p 14). Health and well-being boards [HWBs], the council bodies set up under the Health and Social Care Act that are supposed to link social care with public health and wider health services, are also ignored. They are not even mentioned until page 10 of the MoU, which simply declares: 'Local HWBs will agree strategies and priorities … within their districts and in the context of the GM [Greater Manchester] wide strategy and local priorities.' Many localities will certainly find their priorities overruled by the 'GM wide' bodies that are really in charge. The Greater Manchester Combined Authority (GMCA) has effectively taken over the role of one of the strategic health authorities (SHAs) that were scrapped by Andrew Lansley's Health and Social Care Act 2012, but it will also have control over social care budgets – and quite possibly even less democratic accountability than the old SHAs, since it seems unlikely that the high-powered decision making will take place in open session or publish board papers. A new 'Health and Social Care Devolution Programme Board' will also be set up, with three bureaucrats from the GMCA, three from Greater Manchester's CCGs, an undisclosed number from the 15 NHS and foundation trusts serving Greater Manchester and bureaucrats from NHS England and the Department of Health. The programme, says the MoU, 'will need to be supported by full-time resources … this will include a full-time chief officer, a full-time Finance Director and such other staff as the parties agree' (Association of Greater Manchester Authorities, 2015, p 12). The bureaucracy is already growing. Hence, John Lister asks: 'If the NHS budget is to be controlled by cash-strapped local government, how long before barely adequate, frozen health budgets are siphoned off to prop up social care, or the values of means-tested charges for social care begin to erode the NHS principle of services free at point of use on the basis of clinical need?' Lister concludes:

> A real answer to Osborne's stitch-up is not to go back to
> the post-2012 status quo, but to reinstate the NHS as a
> public service, the way it was before 25 years of market-
> style 'reforms.' That means repeal and reversal of the Health
> & Social Care Act, and the development from the local
> level upwards of new health authorities to take charge.
> (*Morning Star*, 17 March 2015)

Some 20 other areas have submitted health and social care devolution
bids to the Treasury. The King's Fund health think-tank, moreover,
emphasises that 'A key concern is whether the NHS can deliver on
this agenda at the same time as it attempts to tackle mounting financial
and operational pressures' (McKenna and Dunn, 2015, p 17). For
example, GMCA's health and social system faces a deficit of around
£2 billion over the next five years, from 2015 to 2020. Manchester's
mental health trust faces closure because of a £7 million deficit. The
King's Fund report also makes clear that the best available international
research provides no proof that GMCA's scheme will work.

Why, then, does the Tory government want city CAs run by DEMs?
After all, as Richard Hatcher observes, it 'could rely perfectly well
on existing councils to continue to carry out government cuts, as
they have been doing, without creating elaborate new city region
structures'. Hatcher argues that the government's reasons for the
policy are as follows:

1. Local government needs to operate on a scale that corresponds
   to that of the local economy. Individual local authorities are too
   small. For example, the supply chain for Jaguar Land Rover in
   Solihull stretches right across the seven urban authorities in the
   West Midlands, and so does its workforce.
2. Economic competitiveness increasingly requires that every aspect
   of social life, the entire urban process, is harnessed to and integrated
   into the needs of the local economy.

3. DEMs, as previously argued, are the optimal management arrangement for privatised services to increase the rate of profit.

4. Although the central driver of CA policy is economic there are also potential political and ideological benefits to be gained. The devolution of powers to city regions is intended to give credibility to a Conservative discourse of democracy and local empowerment and alleviate hostility to centralised control from Whitehall. It is a strategy to attempt to convince working-class voters in the largely Labour-run CA urban conurbations of Cameron's claim that the Tory party is 'the real party of working people'. The Northern Powerhouse also has the potential to dull some of the pain of cuts: since it can be presented as a radical transformation in the way services and investment are controlled and delivered, with power placed in the hands of northern communities who have felt disenfranchised from the 'Westminster elite' for so long. (Hatcher, 2015c)

Birmingham Trades Union Council (BTUC) agreed unanimously on 4 June 2015 that the West Midlands Combined Authority (WMCA) 'represents a threat to public services, their users and workers, and further undermines local democracy'. BTUC's alternative policies are therefore as follows:

1. no to a DEM;

2. the creation of an elected WMCA Assembly, comprising either directly elected members or councillors from the constituent councils, in either case to be on the basis of proportional representation. (The population of the WMCA would be around 2.7 million. The population of Wales, with an elected Welsh Assembly, partly constituted by proportional representation, is not much larger, at 3 million.)

3. the creation of an elected WMCA 'cabinet' based on the above;

4. a DEM, if imposed, to be subject to the decisions of the Assembly and cabinet;

5. the establishment of powerful Scrutiny Committees at the WMCA level, comprising Assembly members together with lay members including trade union representatives;

6. no transfer of public services such as would put at risk equality of provision on a national basis.

BTUC also called for 'a period of full consultation on any proposals for a WMCA, including a referendum with alternative proposals included' and 'a West Midlands People's Convention to be held in the near future to discuss the proposal and responses to it'.

PWC, while conceding that 'governance structures are important and the issue of accountability should not be overlooked', is adamant that 'discussions about governance should not be allowed to become a distraction' (PWC, 2015, p 13). Yet, as the House of Commons Public Accounts Committee concluded, the DCLG

> did not include a consistent definition for common outcome measures with cities. Therefore, the claims for 25,000 jobs and 10,000 apprenticeships created so far are not based on consistent measurement and are of limited use when trying to distinguish whether any of the reported figures are new jobs, or whether they have moved from one economic centre to another as a result of these policy interventions ... We are mindful of the difficulty of assessing the impact of growth policies over the long term, but we do not accept the Department's explanation that it was too difficult to measure and evaluate key growth outcomes consistently between the cities and across government departments. (House of Commons, 2015b, pp 5–6)

Paul Salveson argues that CAs are 'a recipe for political chaos with a directly elected mayor for the whole of the city region having to work with council leaders whose focus is bound to be very much on their own district and maybe with a different political agenda'.

Salveson concludes that directly elected regional assemblies with similar devolved powers to those of Scotland and Wales would give all parts of Britain broadly similar devolved responsibilities. We also need 'strong, re-energised local government with real power and resources' (Salveson, 2015, p 7), plus the committee system in which all councillors again make policy in much smaller local authorities, in order to eliminate local government's democratic deficit. For example, in France, in greater Lyon since 2014, each party in every arrondissement has appointed councillors who represent the arrondissement at the Grand Lyon Assembly. Seats are allocated to cities dependent on their population size. Richard Hatcher argues that this sort of model could apply in Britain with, for example, 'a Greater Manchester Assembly comprising some councillors from each of the 10 councils on a proportional political and numerical basis' (2015b, p 9).

Pending their abolition, CAs run by DEMs should, as BATC argues, promote 'economic growth for social needs and well-paid jobs, not just private profit'; 'improved public services, not more cuts'; and 'public participation in decision-making, not top-down diktats'. The WMCA has a similar population to Wales and will be run by just the 14 leaders of the seven councils and a DEM – who are almost all male and white. Thus, BATC campaigns for WMCA to also have:

- an elected Assembly;
- co-opted elected delegates from union, community and user bodies on the Board and Scrutiny Committee (which consists of 16 councillors and is scheduled to meet for only two hours four times a year);
- co-opted relevant stakeholders including service users and trade union representatives on the Productivity, Land and Mental Health commissions;
- inclusive and powerful committees for each of the seven Portfolio issues – employment and 'skills', housing, and so on – made up of representatives from wider forums (BATC, 2016).

The Times (22 August 2016) reported that Prime Minister Theresa May was considering dropping the policy of imposed DEMs because she was 'nervous' about giving a platform to senior Labour figures like former minister Andy Burnham, who is the party's candidate for Greater Manchester's DEM. The devolution deal in the North East was scrapped by Communities Secretary Sajid Javid after the leaders of the seven councils involved were split by a single vote on whether to accept a deal that would include a raft of new powers and £30 million a year in return for establishing a DEM (*Guardian*, 9 September 2016). Regional leaders wanted assurances that they would get all their European money from the European Social Fund and European Regional Development Fund even if it is no longer provided by the EU up to 2020 and beyond, but the government would guarantee only projects signed before the 2016 Autumn Statement. Yet many in the North East believe that the European money was merely a proxy for problems that have dogged the negotiation process. Moreover, some of the North East's Labour leaders oppose an imposed DEM. The region has also seen heavy budget cuts, and some of its councils were outraged when in 2016 the former chancellor, George Osborne, granted only Northumberland a tiny share of the £300 million transitional fund designed to cushion the blow of the Treasury funding changes, while other North East councils got nothing. Much of the money went to Tory shires instead, fuelling fears that devolution was simply a way to make councils carry the can for nationally imposed cuts. Clearly the £30 million a year of investment money from the devolution deal will not make up for the £62 million of cuts the North East region's seven councils had in 2016, although on 28 September 2016 *Insider Media Limited* reported that Newcastle, North Tyneside and Northumberland had decided to go it alone.

But the biggest issue – which extends well beyond the North East – as Simon Parker noted, 'is a growing sense of unease about whether the devolution deals are really worth it' (*Guardian*, 14 September 2014). And Jim O'Neill, the former Goldman Sachs chief economist who was appointed to George Osborne's Treasury team in 2015 with responsibility for the 'Northern Powerhouse' project, stepped down as a Treasury minister and resigned the Conservative whip. In his letter to Prime Minister Theresa May he played down speculation that he was unhappy in the job because of her replacement of Osborne's focus on the North with a broader industrial strategy across the whole country (*Guardian*, 24 September 2016).

Note

[1] http://www.kenlivingstone.com/policy

3
POLICE AND CRIME COMMISSIONERS – ANOTHER 'HALF-BAKED IMPORT'

Directly elected police and crime commissioners (PCCs), according to Shami Chakrabarti, are 'a half-baked import from the US, where political "sheriffs" have watched over widespread corruption and damaged race relations for years' (2012, p 21). This chapter discusses the police governance system before PCCs; the Police Reform and Social Responsibility Act 2011; the main arguments against PCCs; why they should be abolished; and what should replace them.

The governance system before PCCs

Following the 1960–62 Royal Commission Report on the constitutional position of the police throughout Great Britain – itself a response to police abuse scandals – the 1964 Police Act introduced police authorities with two-thirds elected members in county or borough councils and one-third magistrates. Several of the amalgamated forces formed under the 1964 Act had short existences, as a wholesale reorganisation of local government in England and Wales outside London was carried out in 1974 under the Local Government Act 1972. Police areas were realigned to correspond to one or more of the non-metropolitan or metropolitan counties created by the 1972 legislation.[1] In the 1980s, especially during the miners' strike, the party-political debate about police accountability was at its height. Tory rhetoric resisted the Labour call for democratic control of policing, invoking the threat of politicisation and defending the strong independence doctrine. However, in the early 1990s, as Labour became 'New' – the era of Michael Howard as Home Secretary versus Tony Blair as shadow – a new consensus around tough 'law and order' developed and has reigned ever since.

The 43 forces in England and Wales varied significantly in terms of population, geographical size, crime levels and trends; and the Police and Magistrates' Courts Act 1994 altered the composition of the authorities in England and Wales, with independent members being added. A long list, compiled from applications received, was submitted by a committee of elected members and magistrates to the Home Office. That committee then appointed the independent members from a short list returned by the Home Office. Typically, a police authority comprised 17 members, of whom nine were elected members drawn from the local authority or authorities for the force area and who would be reflective of the political make-up of those authorities. The remaining eight members were called independent members and were appointed from the local community for fixed terms of four years by the police authority itself. At least three of the 'independent members were magistrates. There was no difference in power or responsibility between the different types of member – there were examples of elected, independent and magistrate members chairing police authorities throughout England and Wales.[2] The bulk of police funding came from the Home Office in the form of an annual grant (calculated on a proportionate basis to take into account the differences in terms of population, geographical size, crime levels and trends), although police authorities could set a precept on the council tax to raise additional funds. The Home Office had the power to prevent any precept increases deemed to be excessive. It was the police authority's responsibility to set the budget for the force area, which included allocating itself enough money from the overall policing budget to ensure that it could discharge its own functions effectively. In its annual Policing Plan, a police authority had to publish its budget for the year, as well as a value-for-money statement, and to outline planned efficiency savings.[3] The previous police governance system had involved a tripartite relationship – the Home Office, police authorities and an operationally independent chief of police or chief constable. Police authorities comprised of local councillors and independent members were intended to provide democratic oversight to chief constables and work with guidelines directed from the Home Office. But police authorities 'rarely held Chief Constables accountable for their actions', 'remained subservient to the perceived greater understanding of both officers and the Home Office' and were 'almost invisible to the public eye, with the vast majority of the public unaware of what they did, or even that they exist[ed] at all' (Roth, 2010, p 9). Policing also became more centralised in the Home Office, which increasingly held chief constables to account.

The Police Reform and Social Responsibility Act 2011

Under the Coalition government the Police Reform and Social Responsibility Act became law on 15 September 2011, following the Bill's ten-month journey through Parliament. Police authorities were abolished and replaced by directly elected PCCs in England and Wales in 41 police areas outside of London. PCCs are responsible for creating a police and crime plan for their area and have the power to appoint and dismiss the chief constable. They also have almost complete control over all community safety spending in the local area and are intended to communicate with people in their community and provide them with information about policing activities and goals. The positions wield considerable power and, excluding in London, PCCs have the largest mandate of any elected official in Britain. The first elections for PCCs took place on 15 November 2012. These PCCs were elected for three-and-a-half years, but subsequently elections are for fixed four-year terms to coincide with local elections, as originally planned.

Oversight for the PCCs is administered by Police and Crime Panels (PCPs) made up of elected local councillors and other independent members. The PCP is a scrutiny body that exists to scrutinise the PCC, to promote openness in the transaction of police business and to support the PCC in the effective exercise of their functions. The Act also makes detailed provisions on PCP composition. These are:

- Where a force area consists of 10 or fewer local authorities, the number of members of the PCP will be 10, not including the co-opted members.
- Where a force area consists of more than 10 local authorities, there will be as many members as there are local authorities in the force area, plus two co-opted members.
- Additional councillors may be co-opted onto the PCP, as long as two lay co-optees are also included, the size of the PCP does not exceed 20 and the Secretary of State approves the co-options.
- Composition should be carried out in accordance with the 'fair representation objective' – essentially, each authority in the force area must be represented by at least one member if the total number of authorities in the area is less than 10, and one member if the number of authorities is 10 or more.
- Where agreement cannot be reached the Secretary of State has the power to make nominations.
- The PCC cannot be a member of the PCP.
- Sitting MPs, Welsh Assembly Members, Members of the Scottish Parliament, Members of the European Parliament, staff of the PCC and civilian police staff may not be co-opted onto the PCP. (Local Government Association, 2011, p 21)

The Act also changed the structure of policing in London. The Mayor, through the Mayor's Office of Policing and Crime (MOPAC), was given the same powers as a US PCC. The MOPAC was established on 16 January 2012 and on 1 June 2012 the Mayor appointed a statutory Deputy Mayor for Policing and Crime (DMPC) to carry out these responsibilities. The MOPAC must secure the maintenance of the Metropolitan Police force, ensure its efficiency and effectiveness and publish a policing and crime plan at least annually. Under the legislation, the London Assembly was also empowered to set up a special-purpose committee, the Policing and Crime Committee, to scrutinise the work of the MOPAC. The Committee can reject, on a two-thirds majority, the appointment of any DMPC who is not an Assembly member, but it has no power to reject the Mayor's Policing and Crime Plan.[4] The City of London Police – tailored to the needs of the City as a tax haven – was unchanged and compounded by the non-residential business vote, which in 2002 was extended following a private act of Parliament submitted by the City of London Corporation itself (see Latham, 2011a, p 87).

Outside London the 41 police authorities in England and Wales were dissolved on 22 November 2012 and replaced with PCCs. Mandatory 'metro' mayors, moreover, will be able to undertake the functions of PCCs in England. The other four police authorities are: the Police Service of Northern Ireland (which replaced the Police Authority for Northern Ireland on 4 November 2001), which is now divided into 11 Districts to mirror the new 'super' local council boundaries; the two special police forces, the British Transport Police and the Civil Nuclear Authority; and the Scottish Police Authority. The latter was created by the Police and Fire Reform (Scotland) Act 2012, which brought together the eight police boards, the Scottish Police Services Authority and the Scottish Crime and Drug Enforcement Agency. The Police Service of Scotland (Police Scotland) became operational on 1 April 2013.

PCCs lead to cronyism and patronage

PCCs are required to appoint a Chief Executive Officer (CEO) and a Chief Finance Officer to assist them in the fulfilment of their responsibilities. The salaries of CEOs range widely, from £61,530 in Durham to £117,762 in West Yorkshire. PCCs are also at liberty to appoint other staff, on merit, as appropriate. Party-political office holders and active party members will not be able to be appointed to the PCC's staff. However, the position of Deputy is not a politically restricted post; and there is no requirement, as in the case of the Chief

Executive Officer and Chief Finance Officer, to advertise these posts. Consequently, some of the first cohort of PCCs recruited political or personal contacts. For example:

- In Greater Manchester the Labour PCC Tony Lloyd (a former New Labour minister, whose annual salary is £100,000), with a staff of 40, appointed his former constituency worker, Clare Regan, as his Policy Adviser without advertising the role.
- In Northamptonshire, the Tory PCC Adam Simmonds (whose annual salary is £70,000) appointed four Assistant Commissioners at salaries of £65,000 each. They include, as Assistant Commissioner for governance, Simmonds' election campaign agent Kathryn Buckle and a second Conservative official as his strategic adviser.
- In the West Midlands Labour PCC Bob Jones (who died in July 2014 and whose annual salary had been £100,000) appointed three Assistant Commissioners on salaries of £22,500 who were all Labour councillors; and his deputy was Yvonne Mosquito, with a salary of £65,000. Yvonne Mosquito is also a Birmingham councillor and the PCP urged her to stand down from her paid role as Chair of Ladywood District Committee. Yvonne Mosquito received a total of £91,841: £65,000 as a Deputy PCC; £16,267 as a backbench councillor; and £10,574 special responsibility allowance as a District Committee Chair.
- In Kent, Independent PCC Ann Barnes (whose annual salary was £85,000) appointed her Liberal Democrat campaign manager, who had no apparent policing experience, as an adviser, with a salary of over £70,000; paid another member of her election team £5,900 a month as an adviser; and paid a former Police Authority colleague £300 a day to be Principal Adviser. Ann Barnes also appointed Paris Brown as her youth police crime commissioner on 4 April 2013. Brown was forced to resign after it emerged that she had posted violent, racist and homophobic messages on the internet. Paris Brown would have received £15,000 a year and the use of a car.

- In Surrey, Independent PCC Kevin Hurley (whose annual salary is £70,000) appointed a former colleague in the Metropolitan Police as his deputy, with a salary of £50,000.
- In West Yorkshire Labour PCC Mark Burns-Williamson (whose annual salary is £100,000) appointed Isabel Owen as Deputy PCC with a salary of £53,000 a year. She is a former Labour parliamentary candidate with no policing experience. The role was advertised only to Labour Party colleagues. Ms Owen is married to Paul Nicholson, regional director of Labour in Yorkshire who oversaw the process whereby Burns-Williamson was appointed the unopposed Labour candidate.
- In West Mercia, Independent PCC Bill Longmore (a former policeman) appointed 'his buddy' and former campaign manager Barrie Sheldon, also a former policeman, as his £50,000-a-year deputy, and was accused of cronyism by the PCP at its inaugural meeting.
- In Humberside, Tory PCC Matthew Grove (whose annual salary was £75,000 and who was a councillor on East Riding of Yorkshire Council until March 2013) appointed East Riding Tory councillor Paul Robinson as his deputy. Robinson angered party colleagues by insisting on remaining a councillor (House of Commons, 2013b, pp 19–21; *Guardian*, 7 December 2012; *Telegraph*, 7 and 17 April 2013).

Therefore, as the Stevens Commission concluded: 'The appointment of staff has ... further exposed the limits of a single individual model of police governance' (Stevens, 2013, p 82).

PCCs lead to corruption

Out of the 50 US states, 48 have sheriffs. Today there are 3,083 elected sheriffs in the US. Moreover, as Patrik Jonsson notes, from the rise of the sheriff, especially in the American West, 'dozens of sheriffs have faced indictments for malfeasance while in office over the last decade for everything from destroying incriminating court documents to murder' (*Christian Science Monitor*, 31 August 2013). For example, former Whitley County Sheriff Lawrence Hodge was imprisoned for 15 years and 6 months in 2011 after pleading guilty to three felony offences (conspiracy to effect commerce by extortion, distribute Oxycodone and commit money laundering); and was ordered to pay $64,897 in restitution to the Whitley County Fiscal Court once he was released from custody and to forfeit $50,000 to the federal government. On 31 October 2013 Hodge pleaded guilty to 18 further counts of abuse of the public trust and three counts of tampering with physical evidence and was sentenced to 17 years in prison by Whitley County Fiscal Court, which were to be served concurrently with his federal prison sentence. He was also ordered to pay a further $335,188 in restitution (*News Journal*, Corbin, Kentucky, 1 November 2013).

Many police commissioners are also appointed by mayors, or city leaders in the US; and every few years, in every major city, there is an investigation that results in the police commissioner and many senior officers being imprisoned. For example, in 2000 New York City (NYC) Mayor Rudy Giuliani appointed Bernard Kerik, a former detective who had been the mayor's driver, as Commissioner. Kerik served 16 months as Commissioner, leaving office at the end of Giuliani's term on 31 December 2001. From May to September 2003 he was then Minister of the Interior of Iraq under the interim US government that ran that country after the invasion. In December 2004 George Bush nominated Kerik to head the Department of Homeland Security, but a week later withdrew his nomination, explaining that Kerik had employed an illegal immigrant. Kerik, who was subsequently prosecuted for fraud, perjury and corruption, could have faced a maximum sentence of 142 years in prison and $4.7 million in fines, but following a plea bargain he was imprisoned for only four years, ordered to pay restitution of nearly $188,000 and released on 28 May 2013.[5] Jessica de Grazia – who served in the New York district attorney's office from 1975 to 1987 and became Manhattan's most senior non-elected law officer –challenges the key assumption underlying the UK's PCC legislation:

> If you are going to take another country's governance system, then you should import the checks and balances from that system. That has not happened in this case. The problem appears to be that they are looking only at crime reduction and not corruption. In the US prosecutors can initiate investigations, while in the UK we are completely dependent on the police. (*Observer*, 6 March 2011)

The Home Office strongly denied such claims, but de Grazia further said she that had been approached by a number of veteran Scotland Yard CID commanders who had experienced police corruption at first hand and were 'horrified' by plans to install an elected commissioner with the power to hire and fire chief constables.

More than half of the first cohort of elected PCCs (23 out of 41) were investigated by the Independent Police Complaints Commission (IPCC) while only half way through their first term (*Telegraph*, 1 December 2014). For example:

- Durham Labour PCC Ron Hogg was investigated regarding allegations that he 'knowingly accepted benefits he was not entitled to' during his time as Deputy Chief Constable of Cleveland Police. The Crown Prosecution Service (CPS) concluded that there was insufficient evidence to warrant criminal charges.
- Lancashire Labour PCC Clive Grunshaw was investigated regarding allegations of false accounting. The IPCC determined that while errors had been made in expense claims, these were due to carelessness rather than any dishonest intent. The CPS concluded that no further action should be taken.
- Kent Independent PCC Ann Barnes was investigated over an allegation of driving without insurance. The CPS concluded that no further action should be taken.
- Norfolk Independent PCC Stephen Bett was investigated regarding allegations of false claims for travel expenses. He subsequently repaid £2,721.60 – the amount that Her Majesty's Revenue and Customs assessed had been overpaid.

These are all examples of what Sir Norman Bettison, the former Chief Constable of West Yorkshire, calls "corruption with a small c" (quoted in the *Telegraph*, 27 February 2012). But, as in the cases of the Westminster Homes for Votes scandal, Jacques Chirac in Paris and Marisol Yagüe in Marbella, corruption on a large scale takes years to substantiate and deal with. Meanwhile, Devon and Cornwall PCC Alison Hernandez was referred to the IPCC on the same day that she officially started her term of office over allegations that she had breached electoral rules on expenses in her role as election agent for Conservative MP Kevin Foster in the 2015 general election (*Police Oracle*, 16 May 2016).

PCCs are a monoculture that excludes the working class

The process of selection and election, as in the case of DEMs, has produced a cohort of PCCs who are predominantly from the middle strata, white, male and middle aged. For example, in the 2012 PPC elections:

- 99 (51.8%) candidates had previously been elected politicians (councillors, MPs, MEPs, Assembly Members) and 25 (60.9%) of those elected had been elected politicians;
- 35 (18.3%) candidates were women and six (14.6%) of those elected were women;
- 20 (10.5%) candidates were from ethnic minorities and none was elected;
- 39 (20.3%) candidates are known to have served on a police authority;
- 32 (16.6%) candidates are known to have been employed by or to have served within the police service (predominantly former officers, but also some Special Constables). Eight of those elected were former officers;
- 16 (8.3%) candidates are known to be or to have been a magistrate and five of those elected were magistrates;

- 16 (8.3%) candidates are known to have served in the armed forces and seven were elected (House of Commons, 2013b, pp 28–9).

The total number of women who stood for the two main parties fell from 21 out of 82 (26%) in 2012 to 11 out of 80 (14%) in the May 2016 PCC elections. In 2012, two BME candidates stood for Labour and one for the Conservatives; and in 2016, the Labour candidate for Derbyshire was the only BME candidate standing for either party (*Guardian*, 18 April 2016). Hardyal Dhindsa – who is also male – was elected as Derbyshire's PCC. There are still only six women PCCs. As Liberty's Policy Director Isabella Sankey noted in relation to the first cohort of PCCs, their unrepresentativeness is still in 'marked contrast to the previous diversity of Police Authorities' (*Liberty News*, 14 November 2013).

PCCs are the optimal internal management arrangement for a privatised police service

A meeting was held in Parliament on 22 November 2011, hosted by the British Security Industry Association (BSIA), to encourage greater private sector involvement in policing at which:

> The wider issue of elected Police and Crime Commissioners ... was also discussed as a potential turning point in the relationships between the police and private security service providers. One of the key roles of commissioners will be to reduce costs and streamline operations within each force, areas which the private security industry can contribute to immensely. (BSIA press statement, 25 November 2011)

The Tory-led Coalition government imposed a 20% cut in Whitehall grants on forces. Moreover, in March 2012 the *Guardian* revealed the massive scale of the plans for police privatisation by the West Midlands and Surrey (two of the largest police forces in the country) who had invited bids from G4S and other major security companies to take over the delivery of a wide range of services previously carried out by the police. The joint West Midlands/Surrey 'transformation' contract was the largest on police privatisation so far, with a potential value of £1.5 billion over seven years, rising to a possible £3.5 billion, depending on how many other forces got involved. It dwarfed the £200 million contract between Lincolnshire police and G4S, under which half the force's civilian staff were to join the private security company that would also build and run a police station for the first time. The existing police authority in the West Midlands, moreover, gave the go-ahead for the tendering stage in February 2012 after a "robust and forthright discussion" that ended with a rare 11–5 split vote (quoted in the *Guardian*, 3 March 2012). Adam Crawford, Professor of Criminology and Criminal Justice at the University of Leeds, argued that:

> Many of the activities proposed for outsourcing … involve contact with the public. This flies in the face of attempts to differentiate between 'back-office' staff and 'front-line personnel' which have been central to arguments in favour of outsourcing on the basis that contracting out the former, will allow police forces to dedicate more resources to the latter … Furthermore, outsourcing may undermine 'total' or holistic policing, notably where different elements of policing are hived off to diverse providers … and outsourced private contractors will not be subject to the same regulation, oversight and accountability mechanisms that exist for public police employees.[6]

PCCs are invisible

As Stevens noted: 'There is little evidence to indicate that this new political office has captured the public imagination, or that PCCs are engaging successfully with diverse communities across their constituencies' (2013, p 81). For example, a poll conducted by Populus in England and Wales (excluding London) for the Electoral Reform Society (ERS) in January 2013 found that only 11% of people could name their PCC. That is, after spending £75 million holding the elections and millions more to staff and resource office holders, nearly 90% of Britons had no idea who their PCC was (Garland and Terry, 2012, p 5). And a ComRes poll for the BBC a year after the first PCC elections showed that 38% of people living in areas where there are PCCs either did not know if there was one, or thought (incorrectly) that there was not; and only 7% knew the name of their PCC.[7] In April 2016 a poll conducted by RMG Research for the ERS still found that 89% of people could not name their PCC, and of those who said they could, 10% actually could not. The figure dropped to just 1% when 18- to 24-year-olds were asked if they could name their PCC, and 5% for 25- to 34-year-olds. Only 4% felt 'well informed' about the PCC election on 5 May 2016, and 1% 'very well informed' (ERS press statement, 30 April 2016).

PCCs have not increased turnout and lack voter support

According to the BBC, nearly 5.5 million votes were cast in November 2012, making the overall turnout 15.1% – the lowest turnout ever recorded in a nation-wide election. This meant that most PCCs were elected by less than 7% of eligible voters, which prompted questions about the legitimacy of PCCs. There are various explanations for the disappointing turnout in the 2012 PCC elections. Research by the Electoral Commission (2013) revealed a significant lack of awareness both of the role of PCCs and of the election itself. Just over a quarter of people reported that they had enough information to make an informed decision about how to vote, while around three-quarters reported knowing little or nothing at all about the elections. The timing of the elections also did not help. Rather than waiting to combine them with the next round of local council elections, and despite the fact that the government had committed to holding subsequent PCC elections alongside other elections, the 2012 PCC elections were held as stand-alone elections in November, outside the normal electoral cycle. Moreover, at the first PCC by-election in the West Midlands, held on 21 August 2014 following the death of Bob Jones, although former New Labour transport minister David Jamieson received 50.8% of the valid votes cast, the turnout was only 10.4%, which was lower than the 12% turnout for Bob Jones in 2012 and the lowest turnout for the 43 PCC elections of November 2012.

In the November 2012 elections the proportion of ballots rejected at the count (2.84%) was higher than for any other nation-wide electoral event in recent years, but comparable to that in some other local contests held using the SV system. More than 5.8 million postal votes were issued, representing 16.1% of the entire eligible electorate. In most areas of England this was a small decrease compared with both the 2011 Alternative Vote referendum and the 2010 general election. In Wales, however, more electors were registered for a postal vote than on either of those previous occasions (Rallings and Thrasher, 2013, p 2). The *Guardian* commented on 23 August 2014 that

> it is hard to see what quality of mandate an elected PCC can honestly claim in these circumstances, especially at a time when the Conservative Party, urged by Boris Johnson (elected as London mayor in a 38 per cent turnout contest) is mulling the imposition of a 50 per cent turnout requirement in trade union ballots for strike action … By coincidence, train drivers on the London tube's Central Line were on strike yesterday, after a 90.1 per cent yes vote in a ballot with a 60 per cent turnout. Like it or not, that's a mandate that any politician would envy.

The second set of PCC elections was held on 5 May 2016. According to the BBC, overall turnout across the 40 PCC elections held in England and Wales was 26.4%, an increase of 11.3% on 2012. Turnout ranged from 17.4% in Durham to 49.1% in Dyfed-Powys (which had the highest increase: 32.7%) and Northamptonshire (which had the lowest increase: 2.5%). The highest and most dramatic increases in turnout were in Wales, where the PCC elections were combined with elections to the Welsh Assembly. Average turnout across the four PCC areas in Wales was 43.1%, only slightly below the 45.3% who voted in the Welsh Assembly elections. South Wales, where one polling station infamously received no voters at all in 2012, came second, with a turnout of 42.5%. However, while turnout in Welsh PCC elections rose significantly over 2012, the persistently low turnout for Welsh Assembly elections may create a natural ceiling for PCC elections in Wales.

The average turnout in England's PCC elections was 24.5%, almost 20 points below the same elections in Wales. The largest turnout in England was in West Yorkshire (33.2%), where local elections were held in all five district councils in the PCC area. In two other PCC areas, Merseyside and the West Midlands, local elections were held across the PCC area and turnout in both cases was relatively high. In contrast, the lowest PCC election turnout (17.4%) was in Durham, where there were no other elections taking place. Likewise there were no other elections in Leicestershire, Nottinghamshire and Bedfordshire, all of which produced low turnouts. Although the average turnout represented a considerable improvement, it was still very low for a national election in the UK: 40 points below turnout in the 2015 general election and lower even than the 35% turnout of UK voters in the 2014 European Parliament elections. As Andrew Defty (2016) noted, 'any variation may have had more to do with the combination of the PCC poll with other elections than with any discernible increase in public enthusiasm for the office'.

Of 1.2 million votes cast across five PCC elections in the West Midlands region, more than 46,000 (3.83%) were rejected. One returning officer said he believed the current first and second preference system was too confusing. In West Mercia, more than 5,500 votes were rejected; more than 5,000 were spoilt in Gloucestershire, 4,000 in Staffordshire, and over 3,000 in Warwickshire (*BBC News*, 15 May 2016).

PCCs have an undemocratic voting system

In the 15 November 2012 elections, according to the BBC, Labour received 1.7 million of the first preference votes (32%); the Tories got 1.5 million (30%). However, the Conservatives won the largest number of PCC contests, 16 out of 41 (39%), as compared to Labour's 13 (31.7%) and independents' 12 (29.3%). Independents therefore performed particularly well; and in Lincolnshire, the second round ended in a contest between two different independents. The success of independent candidates is particularly notable, considering that in six areas no independent candidate or minor party candidate stood. Second preferences largely appeared to favour independents and the Tories. However, it is hard to tell how representative this is, as only 658,492 voters cast valid second preferences (out of the 5,350,041 votes cast).

Five Labour candidates and three Conservative candidates were elected outright in the first round. As no candidate received more than 50% of first preferences in the other 33 contests there was a second count. In 21 (64%) of these the number of voters who were denied any say in the second round was greater than the eventual majority of the winning candidate. For example:

- the winning margin in Essex was 3,686 votes on the second count and 47,220 were disenfranchised;
- the winning margin in Humberside was 2,231 votes on the second count and 51,665 were disenfranchised;
- the winning margin in Lincolnshire was 4,135 votes on the second count and 9,429 were disenfranchised;
- the winning margin in Suffolk was 1,941 votes on the second count and 13,217 were disenfranchised.

That is, the 41 PCC election results in November 2012 replicated those of the 54 local government DEM elections held between 2002 and 2015. In only 17 contests of the DEM elections (less than a third) did the successful candidates get over 50% of the votes cast on the first count, and in 25 (over two-thirds) of the 37 contests where there was a second count the number of voters who were denied any say in the second round was greater than the eventual majority of the winning candidate (see Chapter Two). This is why the STV should be used in all elections, including those for DEMs and PCCs until they are abolished.

The second set of PCC elections was held on 5 May 2016. The number of elections fell from 41 to 40 because responsibility in Greater Manchester now comes within the remit of the Interim DEM Tony Lloyd and elections for the Mayor of Greater Manchester in 2017.

According to the BBC, Labour received over 3 million first preference votes and the Conservatives got only 2.6 million. However, the Conservatives again won the largest number of PCC elections – 20 out of 40, which was four more than in 2012. Labour won 15 PCC elections, which was two more than in 2012 (Labour also has the PCC remit in both Greater London and Greater Manchester). Independents won three PCC elections – nine less than in 2012. Most independent candidates who lost were defeated by Conservatives. However, independents were also defeated by Plaid Cymru (who won their first two PCC elections) in North Wales and by Labour in Gwent. This clearly suggests an increase in partisan voting in PCC elections, but whether this is the result of running PCC elections alongside local elections is not clear. The defeat of independent PCCs by Plaid Cymru in North Wales and Labour in Gwent, alongside Plaid's defeat of the Conservative PCC in Dyfed-Powys, does suggest that voting in the PCC elections in Wales has aligned with voting in the Welsh Assembly elections, particularly on a turnout which closely mirrors that for the Assembly elections. Similarly, in England, several independent PCCs were defeated in areas with large increases in turnout in which a large number of seats were also being contested in several local councils. This was particularly the case in Hampshire and Surrey. At the same time two independent PCCs did win for a second time in similar circumstances, most notably in Gloucestershire. Moreover, in several of the areas in which independent PCCs were defeated there were very few local elections in 2016 – most notably Kent, Lincolnshire, Norfolk and Warwickshire. Andrew Defty (2016) concluded that 'The persistently low turnout in PCC elections means that the long-term future of the role remains uncertain, but the influx of independent Police and Crime Commissioners seen in 2012 seems likely to be a thing of the past.'

In May 2016 only four candidates (all Labour) were elected outright in the first round, as compared to eight (five Labour and three Conservatives) in November 2012. In the other 36 contests there was a second count; and in 35 (97%) of these the number of voters who were denied any say in the second round was greater than the eventual majority of the winning candidate. This reinforces the case for using STV in PCC elections until PCCs are abolished, since in 2016 there were more contests in which there was a second count than in 2012. And in 2016 the percentage of contests in which the majority of the winning candidate was less than the number of voters denied any say in the second round was 97%, as compared to 64% in 2012 – an increase of 33%.

PCCs cannot be removed

South Yorkshire's PCC, Shaun Wright – who was the councillor responsible for children's services from 2005 to 2010 – resigned on 16 September 2014, three weeks after the publication of Professor Alexis Jay's report on child sex abuse in Rotherham. When Labour threatened to throw Wright out of the party, he resigned his membership. Meanwhile Harry Harpham, chair of South Yorkshire's PCP, endorsed calls by the House of Commons Home Affairs Select Committee for emergency legislation to enable PCCs to be removed in 'exceptional circumstances', because the PCP could suspend Wright only if he was charged with a criminal offence that carried a maximum penalty in excess of two years' imprisonment (*Guardian*, 12 and 17 September 2014). Hence, until PCCs are abolished, as argued in Chapter Two regarding DEMs, people should also have a power of recall leading to a new election if their PCC 'turns out' to be 'bad or ineffective'.

Empowered police authorities versus PCCs

The Stevens Commission recommended that PCCs should be abolished and replaced by directly elected local police boards, which it argues are

> A variant of the 'Scottish model' … In April 2013, the Scottish government created a single national police service – Police Scotland – while at the same time decentralising to 32 local policing areas and 353 wards. (2013, p 88)

However, critics say that the merger has been rushed by the Scottish Government to save money, leaving it without any independent democratic oversight. The new single police authority's 13 members are appointed by the Justice Secretary (the Cabinet Secretary for Justice, commonly referred to as the Justice Secretary, is a position in the Scottish Government Cabinet). The merger is supported by Police Scotland's chief constable, Stephen House, who believes the force will be the model for 'inevitable' union in England, and by many, often younger, senior officers. But several departing chief constables have been openly critical. For example, Colin McKerracher, the former chief constable of Grampian, said:

> "The government are saying that this new service will be locally focused. But the one thing that is changing is that there is no local police board able to select a chief constable and style of policing for the area. There will also be no power to hold their chief constable to account. So they are now fairly toothless policing committees." (Quoted in the *Guardian*, 1 April 2013)

Stevens ignores developments following the Health Boards (Membership and Elections) (Scotland) Act 2009, when direct elections were piloted in two of the 14 Health Boards to elect 10 new non-executive directors in NHS Dumfries and Galloway and 12 members in NHS Fife on 10 June 2010. All voting was postal, using the STV system; the franchise was extended to include 16- and 17-year-olds; and candidates' campaign spending was limited to £250[8] each. The turnout was 22.6% in Dumfries and Galloway and 13.9% in Fife. Eligible 16 - to 17-year-olds were significantly less likely to vote than registered voters aged over 18: only 12.9% voted in Dumfries and Galloway and 7% in Fife. In November 2013 the Scottish government abandoned the idea of directly elected Health Boards.[9]

Lesley Riddoch, commenting on this decision, posed the following questions:

> So did the ultra-low turnout demonstrate we have 'too much democracy' … Does the public really not care about health … or think health managers are doing a good job without well-meaning amateurs? Or does the enormous population size of each health board make efforts at democracy well-nigh impossible?[10]

The average population of Scotland's 14 Health Boards is 380,000. 'How on earth could the best qualified, hardest-working health activist', Riddoch further asked, 'hope to be known in such a massive constituency?' For example, Fife (the least responsive pilot area) serves a population of 363,585. 'That's larger than the population of Iceland.' Within this 'locality' there are three Community Health Partnerships (CHPs) – Dunfermline & West Fife (population 139,407); Kirkcaldy & Levenmouth (population 96,894) and Glenrothes & North-East Fife (population 127,284). These 'community' units are enormous – closer to strategic planning authorities, not the intimate, delivery-oriented, community-sized tier of governance that exists in most other European advanced capitalist countries. Moreover:

> If widening board membership was the objective, elections were never going to provide a solution … In Norway, with genuinely community-sized, tax-raising municipalities of

around 14,000 people, election turnouts range from 70–82 per cent and one in 80 Norwegians stands for election. In Scotland, community councils have a tiny average annual budget of £400 and no statutory clout and services are provided instead by large council bureaucracies for an average 162,000 people. These 'local' councils receive most of their cash from central government. Turnout in the 2012 elections was 38 per cent and one in 2,071 Scots stood for election ... The bigger, more remote and more centrally funded the 'local' council, health board or quango, the less the public participate in its governance and the lower the election turnout. Apathy? Not a bit of it. Wrong-sized governance is to blame.[11]

Robert Reiner argues for

> a back-to-basics approach: a truly balanced tripartism, the 1964 Police Act model with adequately empowered local police authorities. This would come closer to a system that could legitimately claim to be democratic.

But he also recognises, as socialists have always done, that

> the problem lies outside policing, in the final analysis. As Tawney suggested in the 1930s, at the start of the last great depression, democracy is more than a matter of elections: 'Is the reality behind the decorous drapery of political democracy to continue to be the economic power wielded by a few thousand – or ... a few hundred thousand – bankers, industrialists, and landowners?' If it does then the prospects of democracy in one institution, especially the police, are dim.[12]

This must be opposed and countered by a programme of democratic accountability and real community control of the police, which would include the following:

1. full trade union and political rights for the police;
2. reorganisation of the structure of local government in England and Wales so that more councils cover smaller areas, each with a police authority made up of elected local councillors, representatives of trade unions and community organisations, with greater powers to control policing priorities and appoint senior police officials to ensure they carry out democratically decided policies;
3. abolition of the City of London Corporation and the transfer of its police force and the Metropolitan Police to more councils in the London area, each with a police authority similar to that in 2 above;
4. abolition of Police Scotland and the Police Service of Northern Ireland and more councils, each with a police authority similar to those in 2 above.

In September 2015 the Tories published a consultation document on their proposals for 'a legal duty to collaborate for the three emergency services' with 'shared governance for police and fire' under PCCs (HM Government, 2015, p 2). But, as the Fire Brigades Union argues: 'The PCC model of governance is significantly less democratic than the current fire authority model, and ... the involvement of PCCs will disrupt industrial relations'.[13] The former shadow home secretary Andy Burnham dropped Labour's pledge to scrap PCCs (*Guardian*, 29 September 2015). And in February 2016 then Home Secretary Theresa May told the think-tank Policy Exchange that, although the government thinks councils are not suitable to run schools, PCCs are suitable to run the police and the fire service. In her speech May also said the she would like to see the PCC role expanded even further – by allowing them to set up 'alternative provision' free schools to support troubled children (*Public Sector Executive*, 8 February 2016).

Notes

[1] http://en.wikipedia.org/wiki/Police_Act_1964

[2] http://en.wikipedia.org/wiki/Police_authority

[3] http://en.wikipedia.org/wiki/Police_authority

[4] http://www.london.gov.uk/priorities/policing-crime/about-mopac

[5] http://en.wikipedia.org/wiki/Bernard_Kerik

[6] http://www.bss.leeds.ac.uk/2012/10/12/the-privatisation-of-policing/

[7] http://www.bbc.co.uk/news/uk-politics-24930039

[8] http://www.gov.scot/Resource/Doc/343289/0114206.pdf

[9] http://www.bbc.co.uk/news/uk-scotland-scotland-politics-24857054

[10] http://www.scotsman.com/news/lesley-riddoch-unhealthy-to-think-big-is-beautiful-1–3183129

[11] http://www.scotsman.com/news/lesley-riddoch-unhealthy-to-think-big-is-beautiful-1–3183129

[12] http://www.law.leeds.ac.uk/research/events/the-new-democratic-governance-of-policing-the-role-and-implications-of-elected-police-and-crime-commissioners.php

[13] http://www.fbu.org.uk/news/2015/10/police-takeover-of-fire-service-will-put-safety-at-risk-warns-fire-brigades-union/

4

LOCAL GOVERNMENT FINANCE

This chapter looks at the financial provisions of the Localism Act and subsequent legislation relating to local government finance; focuses on recent and future trends in public and private sector employment; analyses trends in UK public expenditure; discusses local government finance in the UK; shows that some councils, which have been cut harder than the rest of the public sector, are already becoming financially unviable; and concludes that the council tax, stamp duty land tax and business rates should be abolished and replaced by a system of land value taxation plus a wealth tax and more progressive income tax to fund increased provision of directly provided public services.

Financial provisions of the Localism Act and subsequent legislation

Pay

Since the financial year 2012/13 local authorities have had to publish an annual pay policy statement, which must be approved by a resolution of that authority before it comes into force. The Localism Act 2011 specifies a number of elements that must be covered by the statement, including the level and elements of remuneration for each chief officer; remuneration of chief officers on recruitment, and increases and additions to remuneration for each chief officer; the use of performance-related pay for chief officers; the use of bonuses for chief officers; the approach to the payment of chief officers on their ceasing to hold office; the publication of and access to information relating to remuneration of chief officers; and requires each local authority to define its 'lowest-paid employee', in conjunction with setting out its policy on low pay (see sections 38–43).

European Union financial sanctions

By 2008, over 50% of the domestic regulation concerning local government in Britain originated in the neoliberal EU. The list of council services affected includes community cohesion, social services, regeneration, procurement, performance and environmental standards. Furthermore, Brussels now has the second-highest lobbying presence after Washington; and the EU's current direction, as John Foster (2011, pp 28–9) showed, is 'strongly against the interests of working people' because:

- EU directives commit it to introducing competition into all state-run utilities and services.
- EU policy (*Europe* 2020) commits it to achieving a fully flexible labour force and reducing the level of the social wage and pensions by 2020.
- EU law forbids the use of trade union collective bargaining to prevent the cross-border undercutting of existing labour standards.
- the EU Growth and Stability Pact requires drastic reductions in state spending on social services ... (by up to 20% in most cases).
- the Services Directive, plus the most recent ECJ [European Court of Justice] decision on the cross-border market in health care, will open virtually all remaining areas of social provision to private capital as existing state provision is withdrawn or reduced.

For example, the Scottish government's Scottish Futures Trust (SFT), which aimed to deliver new projects without incurring increased public debt, has been declared unacceptable by the EU. Instead of exposing this reduction of sovereignty, as it would have done if it had come from Westminster, the Scottish National Party (SNP) accepts it. In particular, as a confidential SFT document stated:

> The [EU] restriction means that private contractors and lenders will now pay all the upfront building and project costs, which will be added to the long-term debt of NHS boards, local councils and the road agency Transport Scotland. That debt, plus interest, is then paid off by authorities over a series of decades via regular payments known as unitary charges. (*Guardian*, 27 July 2015)

The result is the same as PPP and PFI – that is, it loads higher long-term debt costs onto public services and increases the profits of commercial companies.

The EU fines policy contained within the original Localism Bill simply allowed ministers to arbitrarily pass on EU fines to councils when Britain's obligations were not met. But, after it became clear that the Tory-led Coalition government would not delete the clauses completely, the LGA and the GLA negotiated with the DCLG and the final Act requires ministers to lay before both Houses of Parliament, on a case-by-case basis, details of every council to which they intend to pass on a fine, including the EU law it has breached and the total of the fine. This will be subject to a vote in both Houses. An independent panel will also scrutinise, and advise on, any suggested fine, with some members of the panel nominated by local government. Hence sections 48–67 of the Localism Act confirm that there is a real risk that EU fines may be imposed; and if local authorities are found to have contributed to this infraction, the government will seek to pass on part of, or all of, a fine. The minimum level fine is €10 million plus a potential daily interest rate until the European Commission is satisfied with compliance. Local authorities may also potentially contribute to non-compliance with four EU directives (air quality, public procurement, services and waste framework).

Council tax

The Localism Act includes provisions for the Secretary of State to set the principles for 'excessive' council tax. The principles for a financial year must be set out in a report, which must be laid before the House of Commons. A duty is placed on the billing authority, major precepting authorities (for example, county councils) and local precepting authorities (for example, parish councils) to use these principles to determine whether their relevant basic amount of council tax for a financial year is 'excessive'. Where they determine that the amount is 'excessive', the billing authority will be required to hold a referendum. Subject to regulations, a billing authority may recover from a precepting authority the expenses that they incur in connection with a referendum held in relation to the precepting authority's relevant basic amount of council tax. The billing and precepting authorities also have a duty to produce substitute calculations that are not 'excessive'. These will have effect for that financial year if the result of the referendum is that the proposed amount of council tax is not approved by a majority of persons voting in the referendum (see sections 72–80).

The community right to challenge and bid

Under the community right to challenge, a broad range of alternative service providers will be able to submit an expression of interest to run a service, with the potential to trigger a council procurement exercise (see sections 81–108). However, as the National Coalition for Independent Action (NCIA) stated,

> the 'right to challenge' ... is specifically intended to open up the 'public service market'. In the absence of any genuine 'enabling and encouraging' of communities to take on services (in fact the reverse is happening as local charities and community provision are being decimated

by cuts), it is the large corporate charities and the private sector which are taking on this role. (NCIA, 2011, p 16)

For example, LSSI, an American firm, early in 2011 set itself a target to manage 15% of British local authority public libraries within the next five years, although it admitted on 28 November 2011 that it had had to scale back its ambitions. However, as it was bought out by Argos Private Equity in January 2015, by July 2015 LSSI held no library contracts in the UK.[1] And, as the NCIA has further emphasised, 'pressure groups, trade unions, the networks that are actually engaging people and supporting them to take action together ... are not just absent from the "big society" picture, they are unwelcome in it and are being attacked' (NCIA, 2011, p 23).

The community right to bid provisions provide extra time for parish councils and local voluntary and community groups to prepare their bid to purchase a listed community asset, should the current owner choose to dispose of it. However, as George Jones told the Communities and Local Government Committee Select Committee in June 2011:

> We don't need a thousand community activists trained by the Cabinet Office and sent out as agents of central Departments to stimulate local activity ... we've already got 20,000 community activists called councillors. I'd have thought, with localism, there'd be more for them to do ... We already have a democratic deficit in this country, when you compare our councillors in relation to the population. Compared with other countries, we're very low on councillor representation. We need more councillors, not fewer. (House of Commons, 2011, p 125)

Housing finance

The Localism Act abolished Housing Revenue Account subsidy in England (see sections 167–175). Under the Secretary of State's Settlement Payments Determination, which came into effect on

28 March 2012, a self-financing valuation of each local housing authority's council housing stock has been made, based on assumptions made about the rental income and expenditure required to maintain each council's council housing stock over 30 years. Where the self-financing valuation for a local housing authority is greater than the Subsidy Capital Financing Requirement (SCFR) determined by the government, the authority must pay to the Secretary of State the amount by which the self-financing valuation exceeds the SCFR (DCLG, 2012, pp 5–6). Moreover, the Tory-led Coalition government increased Right to Buy discounts to £75,000 (£100,000 in London) per home in 2012; and promised that any additional homes sold would be replaced on a one-for-one basis. But by the end of 2014 only 4,800 replacement homes had been started, with many councils claiming they had insufficient funds to build. Since 2012 some 25,000 homes have been sold under the policy, raising a total of £1.54 billion – no small sum when compared to the £1.8 billion 2011–15 affordable homes programme. Nearly £1 billion of the £1.54 billion raised through the sales has not been used to build replacement properties: £358.1 million went into Treasury coffers; a further £363.3 million was used to pay off historic housing debts; and £151.5 million went into councils' general funds. Just £588.3 million was then left for councils to build replacement affordable (not social) rent homes, because the government uses a formula to project how much would have been raised if discounts had not increased. Only the additional cash is used to fund replacement homes. The LGA argues that councils should be able to retain 100% of receipts (*Inside Housing*, 9 January, 2015).

Three councils – Carmarthenshire, Flintshire and Swansea – have already successfully applied to the Welsh Government to suspend the Right to Buy scheme.[2] Labour GLA Member Tom Copley shows that around 800,000 are on housing waiting lists in London, but just 10,300 new units will be built in London by 2023/24 under current plans. This number will be dwarfed by the 16,100 units expected to be sold off if current rates continue. Croydon Council estimated that for the period 2014/15 sales of 99 or more homes a year would plunge the Housing Revenue Account into deficit. Copley therefore concludes that

> local authorities should have a 'right not to sell' council housing if it is deemed not to be in the community interest to do so ... and ... [n]ewly-built council housing should be exempted from right to buy if the borough wishes [it] to be. (Copley, 2015, p 20)

In 2010 the Tory-led Coalition government also cut capital investment budgets for housing associations by 63%; and London's poorest households have been hit by a £70 million rent rise as housing associations quietly switch thousands of tenancies to higher rents to make up the shortfall. About 25,000 homes in the capital have been converted from 'social' housing to 'affordable' since 2012 and thousands more are to follow, under a policy that has sparked tenants' rebellions. Social rents are typically half the market rate, while so-called 'affordable' tariffs are up to 80% of private rents. Many housing associations have exploited the category change to set rents at the highest possible level, with the effect that only relatively wealthy people can afford to live in homes originally meant for poorer tenants. Over half of London's housing associations set the converted rents higher than 70% of the market rate – although others, determined to keep housing genuinely affordable, have charged much lower rents. The system of changing the housing category when new tenants move into a property means that neighbours in identical flats can be paying vastly different rents. For example, during the period 2013–15 London and Quadrant (L&Q) switched more than 3,000 tenancies, thus earning an extra £7.4 million; Circle Housing switched almost 2,500, thus earning an extra £6.5 million; and Notting Hill Housing Trust switched almost 2,000, for a gain of £6.4 million (*Guardian*, 30 March 2015).

Labour's 2015 election manifesto pledged to 'make sure that at least 200,000 homes a year get built by 2020' (Labour Party, 2015, p 45). But there was no mention of how they would be paid for or built, or whether they would be social, private or affordable. Nor was there any reference whatsoever to Right to Buy and the need for a huge expansion in government-funded council housing built by direct labour. The Tories' manifesto pledged to privatise more social housing – councils will be forced to sell off the most expensive third of all properties when they become empty, in order to help fund the extension of the Right to Buy to housing associations (*Inside Housing*, 14 April 2015). The Conservative Party's suggestion that £4.5 billion could be raised by selling high-value council homes to part-fund its planned extension of Right to Buy to housing associations is also highly questionable. For, according to research by Savills, the average value of a social home in England is just under £208,000; but the Conservative Party's plans to sell 15,000 vacant council homes a year, raising £4.5 billion, assumes an average sale value of £300,000. Susan Emmett, director of Savills residential research, said there was "no certainty" that receipts from sales of council homes would be as high as projected (quoted in *Inside Housing*, 17 April 2015). The ratings agency Moody's estimates that housing associations' income will be cut by 7% or £4.5 billion over the next four years; and has changed the outlook for the sector from stable to negative. Furthermore, one of the UK's biggest housing associations, L&Q, is considering whether it can continue developing affordable housing at all (*Sunday Times*, 30 August 2015). Labour-led councils in London argue that the Tories' plans to force local authorities to sell off more expensive properties will wipe out council housing in parts of the capital (*Inside Housing*, 15 April 2015).

In September 2015, the government agreed a deal with the National Housing Federation (NHF) to extend the Right to Buy to most housing association tenants in low-rent homes. Thus the majority of the detail of how the Right to Buy will work is not in the Housing and Planning Act 2016 but in the agreement document.[3] The NHF calculated that 850,000 households will be eligible for the new Right to Buy extension. Shelter then applied the same take-up rate of the first Right to Buy deal in the 1980s (9% of total stock) and estimated that approximately 76,000 housing association tenants will exercise the new Right to Buy by 2020. In addition, by applying vacancy rates to the levels of high-value stock, Shelter calculates that by 2020–21 the number of council homes sold will be approximately 19,000; and that 85,000 low-rent homes that could have been built under Section 106 will not be built because of Starter Homes. In total, therefore, approximately 180,000 genuinely affordable homes for low rent could either not be built or be sold off in the next five years (Shelter, 2015, p 5).

Conversely, from 1 August 2016, when the Right to Buy policy for council and housing association tenants ended, the Housing (Scotland) Act 2014 will prevent the sale of up to 15,500 Scottish social homes for a period of 10 years.[4] The Welsh Government has also now decided to abolish the Right to Buy. The *Legislative Programme for 2016–17* announced that a Bill to abolish the Right to Buy and right to acquire would be introduced during the current session (House of Commons Library, 2016e, p 3). The Northern Ireland Executive is considering halting the Right to Buy for housing associations (*Inside Housing*, 31 August 2016). The 2016 Labour Party conference agreed to reverse the government's 'pay to stay' policy and suspend the Right to Buy (*Inside Housing*, 26 September 2016). Hence the Right to Buy, as in Scotland and as proposed in Wales, Northern Ireland and England, should be abolished; and rent control should also be introduced in the private rented sector.

Business rates

Since April 2013, under the Business Rates Retention Scheme introduced by the Local Government Finance Act 2012, local authorities have been able to keep a share of any growth in business rates in their area as an incentive to promote local business growth. Local authorities as a whole retain approximately 50% of business rates income (the 'local share'). They then pay the remaining amount into a central government pool (the 'central share') to be redistributed to local authorities through Revenue Support Grant (RSG). But since 2013/14 allocations to local authorities have no longer been recalculated annually to take account of changes in relative need, including the ability to raise council tax. Local authorities with rising service needs and low or negative growth in their business rates have had to manage this within their individual budgets (DCLG, 2013, pp 24–6).

Localisation of council tax support

Since April 2013, local authorities have had to implement their own council tax support schemes instead of paying benefits set by the government. Under the new arrangements, the central government funding available nationally to local authorities was 90% of what it would have been in 2013/14. Local authorities have flexibility in how much of the 10% funding reductions they absorb themselves, and how much they pass on as benefit reductions to working-age claimants. To the extent that they maintain existing entitlements they have to find corresponding savings elsewhere; but if they reduce the support given to unemployed claimants – who were previously exempt from paying any council tax – this will increase the cost of council tax collection and arrears.

The Public Contracts Regulations 2015

The UK Public Contracts Regulations 2015 (House of Commons, 2015a) were rushed through Parliament, with the majority of provisions coming into force on 26 February 2015. Unison argues that these regulations should be annulled because:

- they do not make it mandatory for public services to be awarded on the basis of 'best price/quality ratio';
- Regulation 77 on reserved contracts for certain services allows for a wide variety of hybrid and private sector organisations to enter the public procurement market through the use of special purpose provider vehicles. (Roche, 2015)

Private and public sector employment

By Q1 2015,

- employment in the UK private sector had risen by 2.6 million, from 22.8 million in 2010 to 25.7 million – the highest level on a head-count basis since the start of the series in 1999;
- employment in the public sector had fallen by nearly 1 million, from 6.3 million in 2010 to 5.4 million – the lowest level on a head-count basis since the start of the series in 1999;
- employment in local government had fallen by 600,000, from just under 3 million in 2010 to just over 2.3 million. Part of the decrease in local government employment and small increase in central government employment can be attributed to the establishment of the Police Service of Scotland and the Scottish Fire and Rescue Service as central government bodies; these functions had previously been carried out by regional bodies. In addition, schools in England continued to become academies, and when a school becomes an academy its classification transfers from local to central government;
- employment in public corporations also fell by 363,000, from 547,000 in 2010 to 184,000 in Q3 2014, following the transfer of Lloyds to the private sector and privatisation of Royal Mail (required under the EU Postal Service Directive that effectively bans state-owned postal services by depriving them of the profitable business mail and allowing companies to cherry-pick the profitable parts) (ONS, 2015a). Employment in public corporations also fell further in 2015/16: according to the Press Association, public assets of around £31.8 billion (worth more than the previous two decades of sell-offs combined) were privatised. This included the sale of shares in RBS at a loss, sale of the remaining 30% stake in Royal Mail, sale of shares in Lloyds Bank, the privatisation of student loans and other sales.

Within local government, job cuts have had a disproportionate impact on women: 96,000 full-time posts filled by males have gone (21%), compared with nearly 141,000 (31%) filled by women; and 42% (195,000) of posts that have been made redundant were filled by women in part-time employment (Centre for Local Economic Strategies, 2014, p 4). The public sector pay freeze in 2010/11 and 2011/12, followed by a 1% cap between 2013/14 and 2015/16, led to a significant loss in the value of earnings. Analysis by the TUC indicates that public sector workers by 2014 were, on average, £2,245 worse off per annum than in 2010.[5] The Office for Budget Responsibility (OBR) forecasts that

> general government employment will fall by a further 1.0 million by the start of 2020, making a total fall from early 2011 of 1.3 million. That represents a 20% fall in headcount. (OBR, 2014, p 82)

UK public expenditure

The Tory-led Coalition government promised to shrink the deficit that had increased rapidly due to bank-sector bailouts and falling tax revenues. But despite cuts and wage freezes the deficit has risen, mainly due to the failure to achieve economic growth. However, these latter trends seem to be at odds with the figures – often cited by the advocates of greater austerity – showing growing public expenditure as a percentage of GDP (Table 4.1). But, as Reeves et al (2013, p 2) note,

> expenditure as a percentage of GDP is misleading, because GDP (the denominator) has itself fallen, inflating the fraction of spending as a percentage of GDP. Additionally, had the government not pursued austerity policies, spending as a percentage of GDP would have risen even more because of the existence of 'automatic stabilizers' – an automatic rise in overall spending when more people qualify for unemployment benefits and poverty relief during recession (and vice versa when the economy recovers). These stabilizers are so-named because they act counter-cyclically to minimize fluctuations in real GDP.

Table 4.1: UK public expenditure, 1976/77 to 2019/20[1]

	Real terms £ billion	Per cent of GDP		Real terms £ billion	Per cent of GDP		Real terms £ billion	Per cent of GDP
1976/77	359.7	45.4	1991/92	417.3	36.9	2006/07	661.3	38.5
1977/78	346.2	42.5	1992/93	439.5	38.7	2007/08	685.0	39.0
1978/79	353.6	41.7	1993/94	448.3	38.2	2008/09	727.0	42.6
1979/80	361.8	41.5	1994/95	461.1	37.9	2009/10	754.2	45.2
1980/81	365.5	43.2	1995/96	467.9	37.6	2010/11	763.7	44.9
1981/82	369.9	43.3	1996/97	457.1	35.8	2011/12	754.4	43.8
1982/83	381.3	43.6	1997/98	458.6	34.8	2012/13	755.1	43.2
1983/84	394.3	43.2	1998/99	465.6	34.3	2013/14	748.0	41.8
1984/85	398.7	42.9	1999/00	480.7	34.0	2014/15	747.2	40.7
1985/86	393.9	40.7	2000/01	500.6	34.3	2015/16	753.0 plans	40.1
1986/87	394.2	39.4	2001/02	527.1	35.3	2016/17	760.5 plans	39.7
1987/88	396.4	37.3	2002/03	556.8	36.3	2017/18	759.3 plans	38.8
1988/89	385.4	34.6	2003/04	590.1	37.1	2018/19	759.2 plans	38.0
1989/90	396.1	34.8	2004/05	626.4	38.6	2019/20	753.9 plans	37.0
1990/91	397.3	35.0	2005/06	649.4	38.7			

[1] Real-terms figures adjusted to 2015/16 price levels and the temporary effects of banks being classified to the public sector are excluded.
Source: HM Treasury, 2016b, p 65.

For example, the unemployed normally qualify for unemployment benefits, leading spending to rise in parallel. However, the recent budget cuts have broken this historical trend. At a time of higher unemployment there were substantial declines in unemployment benefits per capita as spending failed to keep pace with increasing need. Between 2009 and 2011, the UK increased spending slightly in three areas: social exclusion (mainly comprising Child and Working Tax Credits), housing (increased numbers of persons at risk of homelessness) and pensions (with population ageing). By contrast, spending in all other categories was reduced. This included average annual reductions of £22 per person in sickness and disability benefits, £28 per person in family support (including early childhood development programmes) and approximately £18 per person in unemployment benefits. Cuts to the social housing budget and income support coincided with marked rises in homelessness. Under the New Labour government, homelessness had been declining. But the Coalition government cut housing benefits by 10% for some groups and capped housing allowances, and UK homelessness has since increased by over 40% (about 10,000 additional families). This large rise has occurred despite the Coalition's adopting a more stringent redefinition of homelessness that likely understates the increase. Affordable higher education has been ended with large rises in tuition fees.

In 2014, the OBR stated that:

> Between 2009–10 and 2019–20, spending on public services, administration and grants by central government is projected to fall ... from £5,650 to £3,880 per head in 2014–15 prices. Around 40% of these cuts would have been delivered during this Parliament, with around 60% to come during the next. *The implied squeeze on local authority spending is similarly severe* ... total public spending is now projected to fall to 35.2% of GDP in 2019–20 ... to what would probably be its lowest level in 80 years. (OBR, 2014, pp 6–7, my emphasis)

Yet, as Table 4.1 shows, total public spending is still planned to fall to 37% of GDP by 2019/20, which is less than for Estonia, where public spending, according to the International Monetary Fund, is 38% of GDP, as compared to Finland and France, where public spending is 55% of GDP (quoted in the *Guardian*, 15 April, 2015).

In the Summer Budget of 8 July 2015, as Paul Johnson (2015) of the Institute for Fiscal Studies noted:

> there was only one eye-catching change to the fiscal numbers since the Autumn Statement ... the promised budget balance by 2018–19 ... has now been shifted back to 2019–20 ... [which] does not however represent a let up in the overall scale of cuts – other than for defence.

The OBR also showed that the cuts in central government spending on public services, grants and administration in this Parliament were expected to be similar to those in the previous Parliament. That is, the total cuts between 2009/10 and 2019/20 were now expected to be £120 billion in today's terms (OBR, 2015, p 120).

In addition:

- Only £5 billion would be sought from tax evaders (of £70 billion that is known to exist).
- Corporation Tax would be cut by 2%, to 18% in 2020
- Public sector pay increases would be held down for a further four years, rising by just 1% a year from 2016/17, which the IFS thought would take public sector pay levels well below their long-term average relative to pay in the private sector.
- The biggest single cut to welfare spending would be due to the fact that most working-age benefits, tax credits and housing benefits would be frozen for the next four years; and when inflation was taken into account, according to the IFS, this meant 13 million families would lose an average of £260 a year.
- The next biggest cut came from the reduction to work allowances – the amount that a claimant can earn before benefit starts to be withdrawn – in Universal Credit, which the IFS estimated would cost about 3 million families an average of £1,000 a year each.
- The national living wage of £7.20 per hour for the over-25s since April 2016, as the IFS also pointed out, would not provide full compensation for the majority of losses that would be experienced by tax credit recipients because it was 'just arithmetically impossible … [the] gross increase in employment income from the higher minimum wage is about £4 billion … spending as a whole is due to fall by £12 billion and, even excluding the effects of the four year freeze tax credit spending is due to be cut by getting on for £6 billion … [and] many of the recipients of the higher minimum wage will not be tax credit recipients' (Johnson, 2015).

- The £26,000 benefit cap – the amount one household can claim in a year – would be cut to £23,000 in London and £20,000 in the rest of the country.
- Maintenance grants for students – paid to students with family incomes below £42,000 – would be scrapped and converted into loans from 2016/17.
- All housing benefits for 18- to 21-year-olds would be scrapped.
- The youth benefits systems would be overhauled with a 'youth obligation on 18–21 year olds to earn or learn'.
- Social housing rents would be increased to market rents for those earning more than £30,000 and other social housing rents would be reduced by only 1% in the next four years.

And spending on 'unprotected' services (that is, those other than health, overseas aid, schools and, now, defence) was expected to fall by about a third in real terms between 2010/11 and 2019/20.

Moreover, following the November 2015 Spending Review and Autumn Statement, when the OBR forecast a £27 billion improvement in the public finances over the next five years, Polly Toynbee noted that this

> could evaporate as quickly as it arose and by back-loading cuts previously front-loaded ... the poorest will still be hardest hit by his [Osborne's] £12bn welfare cut, so his tax credit U-turn only delays the pain. Low-earners are his frogs set to boil more slowly, as they shift on to universal credit and take the hit by degrees, while a million of the disabled lose their employment support allowance ... His 'affordable' homes for sale are beyond the reach of all but those above median earnings, the rest of the families consigned to private landlord short-term rentals forever. Don't expect today's good news gloss to withstand five years ahead of real-life state-shrinkage. (*Guardian*, 26 November 2015)

Financing of UK local government

Current expenditure is the cost of running local authority services within the financial year. This includes the costs of staffing, heating, lighting and cleaning, together with expenditure on goods and services consumed within the year. Capital expenditure is incurred when a local authority spends money either to buy fixed assets or to add to the value of an existing fixed asset with a useful life that extends beyond the financial year in which the investment was made. Local authority spending can be divided into revenue expenditure and capital expenditure. Revenue expenditure is financed through a balance of central government grant, retained non-domestic rates and the locally raised council tax. Capital expenditure is principally financed through central government grants, borrowing and capital receipts. The main sources of income for local government in England and Wales are council tax, retained non-domestic rates (non-domestic rates income in Scotland), other government grants (including specific government grants), borrowing and investments, interest receipts, capital receipts, sales, fees and charges and council rents. Most equivalent spending in Northern Ireland is central government spending carried out by Northern Ireland departments.

Total current and capital expenditure by UK local authorities, as Table 4.2 shows, fell from £101.7 billion in 2011/12 to £80.9 billion in 2015/16; and is planned to fall to £69.4 billion by 2019/20 (that is, £32.3 billion less by 2019/20 than in 2011/12). Total current expenditure fell from £90.8 billion in 2011/12 to £70.4 billion in 2015/16; and is planned to fall to £61 billion by 2019/20 (that is, £29.8 billion less by 2019/20 than in 2011/12). Total capital expenditure fell from £10.9 billion in 2011/12 to £10.5 billion in 2015/16; and is planned to fall to £8.4 billion by 2019/20 (that is, £2.5 billion less by 2019/20 than in 2011/12).

Table 4.2: Local government expenditure in the UK, 2011/12 to 2019/20 (£ million)

	2011/12 outturn	2012/13 outturn	2013/14 outturn	2014/15 outturn	2015/16 outturn	2016/17 plans	2017/18 plans	2018/19 plans	2019/20 plans
Current									
England[a]	76,800	71,656	66,239	62,976	58,660	56,105	52,986	51,114	49,631
Scotland[b]	8,764	8,757	7,691	7,315	7,270	6,777	6,853	6,869	6,901
Wales	5,194	5,634	5,717	5,621	4,351	4,201	4,253	4,269	4,288
Northern Ireland	54	59	58	138	147	138	140	140	141
Total	**90,812**	**86,106**	**79,705**	**76,050**	**70,428**	**67,221**	**64,232**	**62,392**	**60,961**
Capital									
England	9,616	8,421	8,009	8,878	8,979	9,170	8,624	8,786	6,943
Scotland	769	607	565	829	880	687	702	733	772
Wales	515	637	569	535	562	583	588	625	666
Northern Ireland	3	3	2	6	46	4	4	4	4
Total	**10,903**	**9,668**	**9,145**	**10,248**	**10,467**	**10,444**	**9,918**	**10,148**	**8,385**
Total	**101,715**	**95,774**	**88,850**	**86,298**	**80,895**	**77,665**	**74,150**	**72,540**	**69,346**

[a] Figures from 2013/14 reflect the changes to funding relating to the localisation of business rates and council tax benefits; [b] Funding arrangements for police services changed following the creation of a single police force from April 2013, which is mainly funded from the Scottish Government.
Source: HM Treasury, 2016b, p 95.

England

Total current and capital expenditure, as Table 4.2 shows, fell from £86.4 billion in 2011/12 to £67.7 billion in 2015/16; and is planned to fall to £56.5 billion by 2019/20 (that is, £29.9 billion less by 2019/20 than in 2011/12). Total current expenditure fell from £76.8 billion in 2011/12 to £58.7 billion in 2015/16; and is planned to fall to £49.6 billion by 2019/20 (that is, £27.2 billion less by 2019/20 than in 2011/12). Total capital expenditure fell from £9.6 billion in 2011/12 to £9 billion in 2015/16; and is planned to fall to £6.9 billion by 2019/20 (that is, £0.6 billion less by 2019/20 than in 2011/12).

Since April 2013 in England under the new settlement funding assessment, all local authorities face the same percentage cut to the main elements of their grant funding each year. This amounts to a greater cut to overall spending power for local authorities that are more reliant on revenues from central government grants than on revenues from council tax – that is, those that have least revenue-raising capacity. The most deprived London boroughs, metropolitan districts and unitary authorities, moreover, have also seen the largest average cuts since 2010. The settlement funding assessment also no longer takes account of the changing needs of local authorities. For example, if one area experiences higher population growth than another over the next few years, this will not be factored into the allocation of spending in future years. Hence areas that see larger population growth will see larger cuts in per-person spending than those that experience lower levels of population growth. London boroughs will be particularly affected, since ONS population projections, according to Innes and Tetlow (2015, pp 31–3), suggest that the eight local authorities with the fastest-growing populations over the five years to 2020 will be the City of London (10.8%), Tower Hamlets (10.2%), Barking and Dagenham (9.6%), Redbridge (8.9%), Barnet (7.8%), Islington (7.7%), Kingston upon Thames (7.7%) and Newham (7.6%).

Between 2015/16 and 2019/20 central government support is planned to fall by £6.1 billion (56%) and locally financed expenditure will increase by 13% (HM Treasury, 2015, p 78). English councils will be allowed to keep 100% of business rates, rather than the current 50%, and to increase council tax bills by 2% to pay for rising social care bills. But they will lose the grant worth £18 billion across councils in England, according to the LGA. Tony Travers from the London School of Economics said that George Osborne's changes were radical because they meant councils would be able to increase revenues in the future only by attracting more businesses, so as to benefit from the changes to rates. He said it transformed town halls from "being a mini-welfare state into a local economic growth agency" (quoted in the *Guardian*, 26 November 2015). This will force councils to sell assets, draw on reserves and raise council tax by £2 billion to prevent the collapse of social care. Moreover, George Osborne's decision to axe the central government grant to councils over the next four years, according to the LGA chair and Conservative peer Gary Porter, is a tragic missed opportunity to protect the services "that bind communities together, improve people's quality of life and protect the most vulnerable" (quoted in the *Guardian*, 26 November 2015). Some of the most stretched councils warned that the changes would hit the poorest parts of the country hardest, where there were fewer businesses and taxpayers to make up for lost Whitehall grants. Liverpool City Council said that its social care bill currently stood at £172 million a year, while the 2% increase in council tax unveiled by Osborne to help fund care for the elderly and people with mental health and other problems would generate only *£3.2 million a year* (quoted in the *Guardian*, 26 November 2015).

Scotland

Total current and capital expenditure, as Table 4.2 shows, fell from £9.6 billion in 2011/12 to £8.2 billion in 2015/16; and is planned to fall to £7.6 billion by 2019/20 (that is, £2 billion less by 2019/20 than in 2011/12). Total current expenditure fell from £8.8 billion in 2011/12 to £7.3 billion in 2015/16; and is planned to fall to £6.9 billion by 2019/20 (that is,£1.9 billion less by 2019/20 than in 2011/12). Total capital expenditure increased from £0.8 billion in 2011/12 to £0.9 billion in 2015/16; and is planned to fall back to £0.8 billion by 2019/20.

The 2015/16 budget cut 1.7%, some £500 million, from total authorised spending of just over £30 billion. This brought total public spending cuts in Scotland since 2010 to around 10% in real terms, with the worst still to come. Over the same period, capital spending had been cut by 26%. However, according to George Osborne's November 2015 Spending Review and Autumn Statement, the application of the Barnett formula meant that Scotland's block grant, which contributes about half of public spending in Scotland, would reach almost £30 billion by 2019/20, a cut of 1.3% per year on average in real terms over the next four years. There would be similar reductions of 1.1% in Wales and Northern Ireland. The Fraser of Allander Institute (FAI) shows that the resource grant is expected to fall by around 13.5% in real terms on a like-for-like basis between 2016/17 and 2020/21. And resources for unprotected areas such as local government could fall by up to 17% if revenues grow relatively more slowly (FAI, 2016, pp 71–2).

Glasgow City Council, on the basis of funding packages offered from the Scottish Government, anticipates cuts of up to £100 million 2015/16 to 2019/20. Highland Council, run by an SNP-led coalition, announced that 1,000 jobs would be shed over the same period, while school days would be made shorter and teacher numbers would be reduced. Labour-run East Renfrewshire, as part of its 'Shaping the Future' scheme to cut £20 million and shed 200 workers, has floated a proposal to drastically reduce the working hours of its school librarians, while encouraging senior pupils to take over the running of the service. While public-sector workers, young, elderly and vulnerable service users bear the impact of the cuts, the SNP budget also includes measures directly aimed at servicing its support base in the management of small-and medium-sized business. For example, the 2015/16 budget statement boasted a reduction in the tax burden on businesses by around £615 million through the business rates relief package. John Swinney, SNP Deputy First Minister of Scotland and Cabinet Secretary for Finance, Constitution and Economy, offered new opportunities for 'reform' of public services by 'partnership working between the public sector, third sector, business and local communities' – that is, further privatisation, semi-privatisation and hiving-off of vital services.[6]

Wales

Total current and capital expenditure, as Table 4.2 shows, fell from £5.7 billion in 2011/12 to £5 billion in 2015/16; and is planned to remain at £5 billion by 2019/20 (that is, similar to 2015/16). Total current expenditure fell from £5.2 billion in 2011/12 to £4.4 billion in 2015/16; and is planned to fall to £4.3 billion by 2019/20 (i.e. £0.9 billion less by 2019/20 than in 2011/12). Total capital expenditure increased from £0.5 billion in 2011/12 to £0.6 billion in 2015/16; and is planned to increase to £0.7 billion by 2019/20.

There was a 3.4% reduction in revenue support grant, to £4.12 billion, for 2015/16 because of 'the large scale budget reductions being imposed by the UK Government'.[7] As Flintshire County Council leader Aaron Shotton, the Welsh Local Government Association's finance spokesman said:

> Local government is no stranger to austerity, with some local services already experiencing budget cuts of more than 30%, but the further £200 million ... means local councils have no option but to look seriously at generating income in different ways and charging for some services ... It is clear to all in local government that the method of dramatically cutting local services will completely undermine their long term sustainability, and the WLGA firmly believes there is an urgent need for a wholesale review of local government finance to be conducted by an Independent Commission.[8]

Northern Ireland

Total current and capital expenditure, as Table 4.2 shows, increased from £58 million in 2011/12 to £193 million in 2015/16; and is planned to fall to £145 million by 2019/20 (that is, £48 million less than in 2015/16). Total current expenditure increased from £54 million in 2011/12 to £147 million in 2015/16, due to the new responsibilities that the amalgamated authorities acquired regarding local planning, urban regeneration, community development, off-street parking and local economic and tourism development (NILGA, 2015, p 7); and is planned to fall to £141 million by 2019/20 (that is, £6 million less than in 2015/16). Total capital expenditure increased from £3 million in 2011/12 to £46 million in 2015/16; and is planned to fall to £4 million by 2019/20 (i.e. £42 million less than in 2015/16).

Most equivalent spending in Northern Ireland, as previously noted, is central government spending carried out by Northern Ireland departments. In June 2015, the 11 amalgamated authorities complained that they were also suffering reductions in grants for waste management, clean air and emergency planning; and also warned that inadequate funding was being provided to cover planning, consultancy and grants to community and arts groups. And there is still more to come, with proposed funding for the amalgamated authorities' new urban regeneration functions falling by more than £12 million. 'Reform of councils should not penalise councils', a Northern Ireland Local Government Association statement said (*Belfast Telegraph*, 26 June 2015).

Councils were cut earlier and harder than the rest of the public sector

Councils are already becoming financially unviable. For example, in May 2013 the House of Commons Public Accounts Committee found that although English councils had £3.6 billion in unallocated general reserves in 2011–12, this was only enough to keep every council in the country going for two months; and 12% of authorities were already at risk of not balancing their budgets (House of Commons, 2013c, p 8). Senior Conservatives in local government, according to Jonathan Carr-West, who is director of the Local Government Information Unit, have for some time been predicting privately that the scale of budget reductions means that some councils, including some large ones, are bound to fail (Carr-West, 2013). Lord Porter further notes that Liverpool is one of "12 to 14 councils that are very close to the edge now". They are not all Labour-led: some of the deepest concerns surround Tory-run Northamptonshire. But, as Liverpool raises only 10% of its total £1.3 billion funding through council tax because of the city's low property values, it is particularly dependent on government grant, which is being cut by 58% between 2010 and 2017. Therefore the council's auditors, Grant Thornton, think it is possible that during 2017/18 the council will no longer have sufficient funds to deliver any discretionary services; and that in 2018/19 it could struggle to fund all its mandatory service provision (*Guardian*, 11 November 2015).

In addition, the 2014/15 local auditors' survey raised concerns about

- 15.9% of single tier and county councils' capacity to deliver their budgets;
- the capacity of 52.3% of these local authorities to deliver their medium-term financial plans, an increase from 41.1% in the 2013/14 survey;
- metropolitan district councils and unitary councils, suggesting that 55.6% and 56.4%, respectively, are not well placed to deliver their medium-term financial strategies. (NAO, 2014, p 21)

The total debt for Scotland's 32 local councils is now £14.8 billion (*BBC News Scotland*, 24 August 2016). This is equivalent to £6,166 per household, as compared to £3,100 per household in England, £2,825 in Wales and £1,213 in Northern Ireland. Some of the key differences from England and Wales are that councils in Scotland run schools to a significantly greater extent, provide social housing directly and also deliver services such as waste management to a significantly greater degree than elsewhere. Councils in Scotland and Wales could lose responsibility for running schools following reviews in both nations. Until April 2015 councils in Northern Ireland, as noted above, were not responsible for local planning, urban regeneration, community development, local economic and tourism development and off-street parking. Annual interest and debt repayments on borrowing in Scotland increased from £946 million in 2009/10 to £1.5 billion in 2013/14. The Non-Profit Distributing model was developed and introduced in Scotland as an alternative to PFI; and repayments for contracts totalled £488 million in 2013/14 and are predicted to peak at around £600 million a year between 2024/25 and 2027/28 (*Guardian*, 5 March 2015).

The system of local government finance is therefore no longer fit for purpose. Moreover, as Mike Turley, UK and global head of public sector at Deloitte, said:

> Two new and significant funding formulas for local government and education have been announced, but both are silent on how they would deal with financial

failure. Deloitte have estimated that over 200 public sector organisations are at risk of financial distress in this Parliament.[9]

Turley is referring here to the new system of local government finance referred to above, whereby central government grants will be phased out, and to the phasing out of council-run schools and the introduction of a new national funding formula from 2017.[10] Nearly nine in 10 councils had to increase council tax and start charging for services in order to balance their books in 2016/17, according to the *2016 State of Local Government Finance* survey, which also found that 82% of councils were forced to use reserves to make ends meet. While nearly all councils that are eligible to do so planned to implement the 2% social care precept, three-quarters of those surveyed said the extra money would not be enough to close the funding gap in adult social care.[11]

In chancellor Philip Hammond's Autumn Statement 2016 (HM Treasury, 2016c), as Jonathan Carr-West noted, there was nothing about devolution beyond the major cities and it was disappointing to hear him blame higher spending by local authorities as a cause of the weaker economic outlook. Carr-West said his real worry was what the chancellor didn't talk about. In addition to no mention of funding for social care, Carr-West (2016) pointed out the absence of any information about how business rate retention is going to work and how local government will be financed in the medium to long term: "This was presented as an upbeat autumn statement, but between the lines there was nothing for local government to celebrate." The next few years will be a challenge for local councils, which face a £5.8 billion funding gap by 2020, according to LGA figures, and difficult decisions about which services are scaled back or stopped. "Even if councils stopped filling in potholes, maintaining parks and open spaces, closed all children's centres, libraries, museums, leisure centres, turned off every street light and shut all discretionary bus routes they will not have saved enough money to plug this gap by the end of the decade," said Lord Porter, chair of the LGA (quoted in the *Guardian*, 23 November 2016).

A new system of local government finance based on Land Value Tax

Land Value Tax (LVT) has a number of advantages, not least that it is a fair tax, since it allows society to reclaim the rising value of land created by the economic activity of society as a whole, instead of it going to the owners of land who contribute nothing to the rising value. Furthermore, it is fair because, in effect, people are charged according to the space that they occupy and its value – and wealthier people tend to occupy more land. In addition, it would lead to the more efficient use of land and eliminate the scourge of derelict sites and homes standing empty, because the tax would be payable whether or not the land was being utilised according to its permitted use. This would act as a powerful stimulus for landowners to develop the land to its maximum potential (in line with prevailing planning regulations). It would also prevent the escalation of land prices, the main element in property bubbles, thus making homes more affordable and leaving more money available for investment, which would provide more jobs, thus helping to promote economic development (Latham, 2011a, p 253).

Recent reviews

Recent reviews of local government finance have also concluded that there is a very strong case for introducing LVT.

- The Burt Review rejected both the council tax and a local income tax for Scotland and 'considered at length the many positive features of a land value tax', which were 'consistent' with its 'recommended local property tax (LPT) ... particularly its progressive nature' (Burt, et al, 2006).
- The Mirrlees Review, which argued that council tax is 'indefensibly regressive', concluded that it should be replaced by 'a housing services tax to reflect its underlying economic rationale as a tax on housing consumption'. Mirrlees also concluded that 'stamp duty land tax should be abolished and the revenue replaced by part of

the housing services tax (for domestic property) and land value tax (for business property' (Mirrlees, 2011, pp 404–5).

- The Poverty Alliance's *Local Taxation Discussion Paper* (2013) considered that 'much of the analysis' by the Burt Review was 'sound', and concluded that 'a Land Value Tax would have been a superior solution so that the LPT, or more correctly the underpinnings for that development, should have led logically onto a proposal for further change along the lines of a land-based taxation'. This paper also proposed that 'a wealth tax should be introduced, first as a one-off move to reverse the significant gains made by the richest during the recession and to raise revenues to begin to address the austerity cuts of the current period' (Cooper et al, 2013, pp 5 and 11). The same authors also had previously argued that in the longer term the council tax should be replaced with LVT (Cooper, et al, 2010).

- *Taxing an Independent Scotland*, by the Institute for Fiscal Studies (2013), noted that the Scottish Parliament had failed to introduce 'the more thoroughgoing rationalisation proposed' by the Mirrlees Review, 'which would involve making council tax a simple proportion of property value … and replacing business rates with a land value tax on non-residential land' (Adam et al, 2013, p 11).

- The GLA's Planning Committee, in a February 2016 report signed off by its three Labour and two Conservative members, concluded that the current property taxation system encourages 'inefficient land use', deters development and makes 'land banking more likely'. They argued that 'LVT has the potential to overcome these drawbacks and deliver higher levels of development to fund London's growth'. Therefore they recommended that the next Mayor should establish what powers are necessary to implement and operate LVT to replace council tax, business rates and stamp duty land tax; should commission an economic feasibility study to establish the likely yields of LVT compared with the existing property taxes, and estimate the impact of LVT on different land uses within the area; and should, subject to the outcome of the feasibility study, trial LVT in an area of London to test the impact of this approach on encouraging and funding development (Copley, 2016, pp 7–8).

The broad alliance of support for LVT

There is now a broad alliance of support across the political spectrum for LVT. Of the major parties, only the Conservatives lack a campaign group promoting LVT, although Nicholas Boles, ex-Minister of State for Skills, supports LVT if 'farmland and people's main homes are wholly exempt' (*Financial Times*, 29 September 2011). The Labour Land Campaign promotes LVT within the Labour Party and across the broad Left movement; and LVT is now the policy of the Co-operative Party, the Communist Party of Britain, the Labour Representation Committee, Compass and Glasgow's Labour Council. Andy Burnham and Diane Abbott, when they were Labour leadership election candidates, supported LVT (Latham, 2011a, p 276). Both Jeremy Corbyn and John McDonnell support LVT. The 2011 annual conference of the Trades Union Congress supported 'an economic strategy that explores the benefits of land value taxes, delivers a peace dividend through the scrapping of Trident replacement and takes key drivers of economic growth and wealth creation back into public ownership'.[12] Mark Drakeford – Welsh Minister for Health and Social Services who is also Professor of Social Policy and Applied Social Sciences at Cardiff University and the main architect of the devolved administration's centre-left policies – told a Labour grassroots fringe meeting at Welsh Labour's annual conference in March 2013 that the party could address the country's fiscal shortfall equitably by measures such as a financial transactions tax, a land value tax, a more progressive National Insurance system, a minimum taxation level and serious efforts to close the 'tax gap'.[13] At Unison's Local Government Conference on 17 June 2013, Glen Williams from the service group executive, – when proposing a motion on council tax benefit, called for consideration of 'a land value tax'.[14] The former Scottish Labour leader Johann Lamont voiced tentative support for LVT; and the Scottish TUC is 'currently researching alternatives to the Council Tax ... appraisal of the benefits and disadvantages of LVT and other alternative forms of taxation is central to this process' (*Scotsman*, 22 September 2013).

Support for LVT also extends well beyond the labour and trades union movement. For example, establishment luminaries such as Sir Samuel Brittan and Martin Wolf of the *Financial Times* support LVT. Liberal Democrat Action for Land Taxation and Economic Reform (ALTER) promotes LVT within the Liberal Democrat Party. Furthermore, in December 2008 a cross-party group called the Coalition for Economic Justice was established to campaign for the introduction of LVT (Latham, 2011a, p 110). Academic supporters of LVT include the Centre for Research on Socio-Cultural Change (see Ertürk et al, 2011, pp 22, 32 and 36–7). Iain McLean, Professor of Politics at the University of Oxford and a member of the independent expert group set up by the Calman Commission on Scottish Devolution, supports LVT, as does Professor Prem Sikka, who also argues for major redistribution of wealth and income (see Latham, 2011b, p 111 and Sikka, 2011, p 9). As Professor Danny Dorling (2014, p 75) argues:

> A land tax means there is less economic sense in one family owning as many homes and as much land as possible, as it becomes more expensive to own more than you need. After the tax has been applied, housing will be valued more for its 'use' than for its 'exchange' value.

Implementing LVT

LVT, as the Labour Land Campaign (2011, p 10) states,

> should be applied to all land. And in order for it to realise its true economic potential and contribute fully towards a more just society, the ultimate goal must be for LVT to replace the Council Tax, the National Non-Domestic Rates, Stamp Duty Land Tax, and to some extent other

taxes, including Income Tax for most people by raising the threshold before tax is paid on incomes.

However, if a pure LVT regime were introduced immediately, people in large, expensive houses and people in smaller houses occupying land of equal value would pay the same tax. This could be avoided if a split tax regime, in which the land value and buildings were taxed separately, were introduced. In order to obtain the £23,964 billion raised by the council tax in England in 2014/15 (DCLG, 2016, p 7), the combined rate of land value and buildings tax would need to be approximately 1% of capital value. But as land prices fell there would be an option to gradually shift more of the tax onto the land value element. Only freeholders and landlords would pay LVT and buildings tax; and the owners of large estates would pay more because their acreage is greater than a semi-detached property and they often own valuable sites in town and city centres. Under this proposal would tenants no longer be liable to property taxes.

Business rates should be replaced immediately by a pure LVT, which would not only be less costly to assess but also less likely to penalise businesses seeking to improve their premises; and it would also stimulate the most productive use of the land, subject to planning consent. Similarly, agricultural land, which is untaxed, should be valued and taxed at the same rate as for other businesses. This would stop agricultural subsidies feeding into land prices and rents at the expense of investment in agriculture and its diversification. And stamp duty land tax, which is in fact a transaction tax, should also be abolished because it adds costs and acts as a disincentive for those wishing to move to somewhere more suitable for their needs.

Should then LVT be a national tax that is redistributed back to local authorities on a per capita basis or solely a local tax? The advantage of the former is that it would enable a more equitable distribution of the revenue that otherwise would be distorted by Britain's highly unequal society. Its disadvantage is that it divorces the collection of tax from the services provided by local authorities and undermines the relationship and accountability of local politicians to those whom they represent. However, local politicians would still be answerable to their constituents for how the funds at their disposal were spent. A reasonable compromise could therefore be for local authorities to retain up to a third of the revenue collected, with the rest going to central government (or the devolved governments in the case of Scotland, Wales and Northern Ireland), which would then be redistributed back to local authorities on a per capita basis.

Notes

[1] http://www.publiclibrariesnews.com/campaigning/privatized-libraries-outsourcing-library-services/lssi

[2] http://www.localgov.co.uk/ 18 November 2015

[3] http://nationalhousingfederation.newsweaver.com/icfiles/1/55885/161177/5359868/a266db71336fb8bfef6fbbf2/rtb%20offer%20final%20fed_2.pdf

[4] http://www.localgov.co.uk/Right-to-Buy-scrapped-in-Scotland/36619, 26 June 2014

[5] https://www.tuc.org.uk/industrial-issues/public-sector/pay-fair-campaign/public-sector-workers-lose-out-per%20centC2per%20centA32245-under

[6] http://news.scotland.gov.uk/Speeches-Briefings/UK-Autumn-Budget-Statement-and-Local-Government-Finance-Settlement-1359.aspx

[7] Quoted in http://www.publicfinance.co.uk/news/2014/10/welsh-councils-warn-of-impact-of-spending-cuts/

[8] Quoted in http://www.walesonline.co.uk/news/wales-news/welsh-councils-face-average-funding-8263918

[9] http://www.ukbudget.com/newsroom-autumnstatement-2015/spending-review-2015-pace-of-public-service-change-set-to-quicken.aspx?linkId=19048478

[10] http://www.localgov.co.uk/Spending-Review-Osborne-to-phase-out-council-run-schools/39905

[11] http://www.localgov.co.uk/Local-government-finance-in-a-mess-warns-survey/40336).

[12] http://www.tuc.org.uk/about-tuc/congress-2011/2011-congress-decisions

[13] http://www.leftfutures.org/2013/03/the-left-frames-the-debate-at-welsh-labour-conference/

[14] http://www.Unison.org.uk/news/articles/conference-hears-council-tax-benefit-changes-are-not-cricket

5

TOWARDS A NEW BASIS FOR FEDERAL, REGIONAL AND LOCAL DEMOCRACY

This final chapter argues that the Marxist approach in political science is still relevant; further deconstructs the European Union dimension; concludes that in order to implement the policy proposals made in Chapters One to Four a new system of federal, regional and local democracy is needed; assesses the current balance of political forces in the UK; and discusses the crisis of working-class political representation and ways in which it is now beginning to be addressed.

The continuing relevance of the Marxist approach in political science

Jonathan Davies, seeking to explain the contradiction between New Labour's ostensible commitment to 'devolving power' and its strong centralising/controlling approach to local government, notes that Antonio Gramsci used the term 'passive revolution' to refer to 'a movement seeking to carry out transformation by non-revolutionary means within the confines of capitalism' (Davies, J.S., 2011, pp 106–7). For example, during the New York fiscal crisis in 1975 a powerful cabal of investment bankers pushed the city into technical bankruptcy and debt payments were funded by wage freezes, cuts in employment and welfare, plus service-user fees. Hence, 'Powerful economic actors mobilised in the face of a crisis of profitability, increasing competition and declining confidence in the city's ability to pay its debts' (Davies, J.S., 2011, p 109). Subsequently, other major US cities (including Cleveland in 1978 and Philadelphia in 1991) teetered on the edge of bankruptcy before brokering similar deals. Moreover, Detroit, the biggest US city to take such drastic action, formally filed for bankruptcy in 2013 when it was faced with debts of $18.5 billion (*Guardian*, 15 July 2013). Davies therefore concludes that

> the power structures of capitalist political economy ... must be confronted at the point of production, distribution and exchange. The question then is whether it is possible to create a movement capable of doing so spearheaded by the organised working class or some other constellation of forces ... the student movement ... and its trade union counterpart ... form a vital part of the terrain upon which the emancipatory potential and limits of networked resistance will be determined. (Davies, J.S., 2011, p 148)

Professor Robin Hambleton (2016, p 13), as does this study, shows that the Tories', despite their rhetoric, are 'pursuing a policy of centralisation on steroids' that will 'decentralise blame, nicely ahead of time, for the truly massive spending cuts that the government plans to impose on local government in the next four years'. Examples of 'centralisation on steroids' cited by Hambleton include the Education and Adoption Act 2016, which will not devolve power to head teachers, as ministers claim, because it will pass to 'relatively invisible and unaccountable trusts' who will 'not need to include parent-governors'; and the misnamed Cities and Local Government Devolution Act 2016, which offers groups of local authorities the opportunity to put forward proposals for increasing the power of their city region or sub-region. The government claims that such legislation is designed to strengthen local government. But under the latter Act, as also shown in Chapter Two, 'ministers get to pick and choose which localities are to be granted extra powers, ministers decide the criteria to be used in assessing bids, ministers review area-specific proposals on a case-by-case basis and, astonishingly, these so-called devolution deals are being negotiated behind closed doors' (Hambleton, 2016, p 12).

Hambleton's analyses are based on international global research carried out for his book *Leading the Inclusive City* (2014), which argues that any authentic devolution of power to localities must pass two tests. First, do the elected local authorities have constitutional protection from interference by higher levels of government? Second, do the elected local authorities have a range of substantial tax-raising powers? The Cities and Local Government Devolution Act 2016 fails both these fundamental tests. Hambleton also urges local leaders in the UK to look abroad to countries where meaningful devolution is well established: for example, in Germany, Sweden and the US.

However, the recall provisions for German DEMs have not prevented rampant privatisation in Germany, where the strategy to outsource and privatise the provision of public services has whittled away the scope of politically decided local issues, thus depoliticising the local area and hollowing out the recent advances in local democracy. Moreover, policies introduced by the federal and Länder governments have deprived local authorities of some key traditional responsibilities, particularly in social assistance, long-term care and labour markets, due to EU-promoted marketisation. The process of hiving-off and corporatisation has also been extended to an ever-wider range of local government functions and activities, including cultural and recreational facilities, and also internal administrative operations, such as planning, accounting and data processing. Now about half of all German local government personnel are employed in such corporatised structures outside the core municipal administration (Latham, 2011a, pp 112–13). And the UK outsourcing market, as was shown in Chapter One, is now the second-largest in the world outside the US.

Similarly, Chapter One also showed that the Tory government is not interested in whether public service mutuals will exist in five years' time, just so long as they form a useful vehicle for the break-up of the public sector. Moreover, as was noted in Chapter Four, under the community right to challenge, local charities and community provision are being decimated by cuts and the large corporate charities and the private sector are taking on their role. And, as the NCIA emphasises, pressure groups, trade unions, the networks that are actually engaging people and supporting them to take action together are not just absent from the 'big society' picture, they are unwelcome in it and are being attacked.

In Latin America the key actors developing new participatory spaces are social movements mobilising for greater inclusion with the backing of political actors. For example, Participatory Budgeting, launched 25 years ago in the city of Porto Alegre, in southern Brazil, was designed to put all neighbourhoods on an equal footing, with equal access and opportunity. In addition, the goal was to deepen democracy by giving residents not just voice but decision-making power (see Latham, 2011a, pp 333–8). Even though city budgets struggle – desperately these days – to cover basic necessities, a 1% or smaller set-aside is sufficient to start the process. Participatory Budgeting has been the centrepiece for building participatory democracy under the leadership of the Workers' Party in Brazil, from 2003 to the present. In Canoas, the neighbouring industrial city, the Participatory Budget was not introduced until 2009, with the election of the Workers' Party mayor Jairo Jorge. Since 2009, the people of Canoas have selected 117 projects, involving 86,000 residents, which amounts to 10% of the voting public. That is the highest Workers' Party participation rate in all of Brazil. At the World Social Forum in Porto Alegre in January 2016, two major panels focused on the importance of promoting the direct participation of urban residents in government decision making. Mayor Jairo Jorge's book exhorts the Left in particular, but all progressives, to *Radicalizar la Democracia:* 'We must engage citizens increasingly in ... governments, giving them decision-making power over investments, public policies and strategic development projects at the city, state and national levels' (quoted in Needham, 2016). Radicalising democracy is the Workers' Party's answer to neoliberal policies and growing inequalities.

The situation in the UK is very different. New participatory spaces emerged from an essentially top-down project to re-engage people. Thus in both Bradford and Manchester the forums were dominated by paid workers rather than activists, as part of New Labour's governance project that accelerated the neoliberal reforms imposed on public services by its predecessors under the guise of 'consumer choice' (see Latham, 2011a, pp 338–9). According to the *Open Public Services* White Paper, people should also 'use their voice in designing and managing the services they use ...' (HM Government, 2011, p 11), which has resulted in councils offering consultations on which services to cut. The WMCA has a similar-sized population to that of Wales and will be run by just the 14 leaders of the seven councils and the DEM – who are almost all male and white. Hence BATC campaigns for an elected Assembly; co-opted elected delegates from union, community and user bodies on the Board and Scrutiny Committee; co-opted relevant stakeholders including service users and trade union representatives on the Productivity, Land and Mental Health commissions; and inclusive and powerful committees for each of the seven Portfolio issues – employment and 'skills', housing and so on – made up of representatives from wider forums'. Yet, without at least the election of a social democratic government committed to the alternative economic and political strategy outlined below, BATC's aims and the proposals to enhance, strengthen and reform local democracy listed below will not be achieved.

Chapter Four cites NAO reports relating to the financial viability of local councils. The relevance of the Marxist approach is demonstrated by Stewart Smyth and Dexter Whitfield (2016), who analysed the contents of the NAO's 2012 report titled *Equity Investment in Privately Financed Projects*. They draw on Gramsci's distinction between 'common sense' and 'good sense' ideas: the two elements of contradictory consciousness, which are dialectically related in a whole, one drawn from the official notions of the rulers, the other derived from an oppressed people's practical, although mediated, experience of social reality. Gramsci also stresses that common sense/good sense applies to all classes. In the Smyth and Whitfield paper common-sense ideas are represented by the adoption and acceptance of market relations in equity transactions and profit making on such transactions as a positive development. In contrast, good-sense ideas are represented by challenges to the appropriateness of such transactions involving public assets. The authors conclude that in the case of this report, the NAO has become an active participant in maintaining the hegemony of competitive market principles as the basis of resource allocation for public infrastructure projects:

> Because they have refused to move beyond the dominant ideology of competitive market principles, the NAO have reached the limit of their ability to analyse and explain what is actually occurring in the PPP equity market ... [they] are aware of the excessive profit-making, but know that they cannot openly report it. Instead, we are left with 'unexplained residual amounts' ... Gramsci's common/good sense ideas opens the space for the work completed by academics that are critical of government policy on PPPs to have a real impact ... the good sense ideas can be picked up and amplified by social movements and civil society organisations (such as trade unions).

The offshore secondary market is a £17.1 billion industry buying and selling equity in PFI/PPP project companies. The three-way profit gain – original Special Purpose Vehicle (a subsidiary company with an asset/liability structure and legal status that makes its obligations secure even if the parent company goes bankrupt), shareholders, secondary market fund sales and shareholder dividends of secondary market funds – means that the total annual rate of return could be between 45% and 60%: three to five times the rate of return in PFI/PPP final business cases. The five largest listed offshore infrastructure funds made a total profit of £1.8 billion in the five-year period 2011–2015 and paid no tax. The PFI/PPP programme should therefore be terminated and replaced by direct public investment, the average cost of which is 3% to 4%, compared with an estimated financing cost of 7% to 8% for all private finance projects (Whitfield, 2016, pp 6–9).

Davies (2011, pp 139–42) distinguishes between 'critical insider' and 'critical outsider' political science perspectives, and emphasises that they are 'not necessarily mutually exclusive'. Hambleton has been an adviser to UK local government ministers, an adviser to select committees of the UK Parliament, and has written national guidance documents for councils in England, Wales and Scotland. Professor George Jones and Professor John Stewart – the leading liberal-democratic academic critics of the Localism Act 2011 and the Tories' latest legislation – are also 'critical' insiders. However, they all fail to acknowledge that mayors with cabinets are the optimal internal management arrangement for privatised local government services. Hence, although the exemplary empirical findings of these and other 'critical insider' analysts are cited in this book, the main problem with such studies is that (unlike this study and other 'critical outsider' analyses such as those by Jonathan Davies, Richard Hatcher and Dexter Whitfield, which are grounded in Marxist political economy and Antonio Gramsci's theory of the 'historic bloc') they do not see such policies as attempts by the central state to restore the conditions in which profitable investment and capital accumulation can take place – although political-office holders, as Ralph Miliband in his later work noted, cannot appear to simply be the agents of capital. Hence, in order to defend the interests of political-office holders effectively, governments must have a degree of autonomy in deciding how this is done (see Latham, 2011a, p 50). For example, the Localism Act 2011 allowed councils to revert to the committee system, which 13 in England have done (see Chapter One). And the Northern Powerhouse – in order to dull some of the pain of cuts – is presented as a radical transformation of the way in which services and investment are controlled and delivered, with power placed in the hands of northern communities who have felt disenfranchised from the 'Westminster elite' for so long (see Chapter Two).

Further deconstructing the European Union dimension

> Institutional protection of the market economy from democratic interference has advanced greatly in recent decades … Economic policy has widely been turned over to independent – i.e., democratically unaccountable

– central banks concerned above all with the health and goodwill of financial markets. In Europe, national economic policies, including wage-setting and budget-making, are increasingly governed by supranational agencies like the European Commission and the European Central Bank that lie beyond the reach of popular democracy. (Streeck, 2014, pp 43–4)

Most worrying of all, the Transatlantic Trade and Investment Partnership (TTIP) seeks to grant foreign investors a new right to sue sovereign governments in front of ad hoc arbitration tribunals for loss of profits resulting from public policy decisions (Hilary, 2014). However, on 28 August 2016, Sigmar Gabriel, who is German Chancellor Angela Merkel's deputy and economy minister, said that no agreement could be reached on any of the 27 chapters of the proposed deal after 14 rounds of behind-closed-doors bargaining. But the UK remains at risk from a similar deal – the Canadian–European Comprehensive Economic and Trade Agreement (CETA) – which the prime minister wishes to push through before Britain leaves the EU (*Global Justice Now News*, 29 August 2016).

In January 2016 Jeremy Corbyn had told Labour councillors that he would use the EU referendum to press for a "real social Europe"; and six Labour MPs launched Labour Leave to campaign for a Left exit from the EU (*Morning Star*, 10 June 2016). The Leave.eu campaign signed up over 500 Conservative councillors – 132 of whom wrote to David Cameron on 12 February 2016 urging him to campaign for Brexit and to 'consider the long-term future of the Conservative Party'. As John Foster concluded in February 2016:

The EU's imposition of neo-liberal policies on all governments, including those led by the traditional parties of the Left, has resulted in the collapse of support for social democracy ... *This is why it is so important that a clear progressive case is put for regaining our full democratic rights – rights to implement policies that can win democratic control of*

*the economy and secure solidarity and collectivism for all working
people whatever their origin and ethnicity.* (Foster, 2016, pp 2
and 34, his emphasis)

On 11 April 2016 a left-wing anti-EU campaign group dubbed Lexit
was set up by rail union RMT, Trade Unionists Against the EU, the
Communist Party of Britain, the Indian Workers Association (GB), the
Bangladeshi Workers Council of UK, Scottish Left Leave, Counterfire
and the Socialist Workers Party (*Morning Star*, 13 April 2016). Lexit
then held a series of rallies across the UK to promote the 'working
class, left-wing and internationalist case' for voting to leave the EU –
none of which was reported by the mainstream media.

The national turnout in the referendum on UK membership of
the EU on 23 June 2016 was 72.2%; the number of ballot papers
rejected totalled 25,359; the total number of ballot papers counted
was 33,577,342; 48.1% (16,141,241) voted to remain; and 51.9%
(17,410,742) voted to leave (Electoral Commission). In England,
the turnout was 73%; 53.4% (15,188,406) voted to leave; and 46.6%
(13,266,996) voted to remain. London (where the turnout of 69.8%,
despite torrential rain and flooding in parts of the city, was the
highest since the 1950 general election, when more than 80% voted)
was the only region in England to vote overwhelmingly to remain:
59.9% (2,263,519) voted to remain, while 40.1% (1,513,232) voted
to leave. Hillingdon, Sutton, Bexley, Barking and Dagenham, and
Havering voted to leave; and the other 27 London boroughs plus the
City of London voted to remain. This was in stark contrast to other
regions in England, which all voted to leave, as did Wales, where the
turnout was 71.7%, with 52.5% (854,572) voting to leave and 47.5%
(772,347) voting to remain. Only Scotland (turnout 67.2%, with 62%
[1,661,191] voting to remain and 38% [1,018,322] voting to leave)
and Northern Ireland (turnout 62.9%, with 55.8% [440,437] voting
to remain and 44.2% [349,442] voting to leave) voted to remain.
That is, only 41.7% of the Scottish electorate (3,988,492) and only
34.9% of the Northern Irish electorate (1,260,955) voted to stay in
the EU. David Cameron then decided to step down as both Prime

Minister and an MP; and Nicola Sturgeon told the BBC that, as she was "absolutely determined" to keep Scotland in the EU, a second Scottish independence referendum was now "highly likely", even though the SNP will

> face significant economic, legal and political questions about leaving the UK. With the collapse in oil prices but high levels of public spending, it has a structural deficit of £15bn, and a weak economy hovering close to recession. It would need to strike a deal with London about paying off its share of the UK's £1.6tn debt. It would also face losing Scotland's share of the UK rebate, having to find the cash needed for Scotland's contribution to the EU, and require the EU's agreement on its currency. EU members may expect Scotland to join the euro. (*Guardian*, 25 June 2016)

Meanwhile most MPs are angry and disappointed at the referendum result. So are millions of people. But even greater numbers did vote Leave, and Labour must respect that if it is to help chart a new course for Britain. Moreover, as Paul Mason (*Guardian*, 5 July 2016) noted, in Sheffield – where there are two big universities and a large population of graduates who have stayed on, plus two big teaching hospitals and a significant number of high-skilled manufacturing jobs – 51% voted Leave, showing that Brexit had achieved what Antonio Gramsci called 'ideological hegemony'.

The leave vote was also in part a rejection of the prevailing neoliberal orthodoxy, and reflected huge anger at the political elite and unaccountable and pro-corporate nature of the EU. According to Lord Ashcroft's poll of 12,369 referendum voters, the most important issue for half of all Leave supporters was sovereignty – that is, that decisions about Britain should be taken in Britain. Only one-third put control over immigration first, although both sovereignty and immigration as well as the economy were important to the majority of anti-EU voters. However ill-founded it may be, concern about the impact of immigration on local jobs, wages and public services is not a sure-fire indicator of racism. Just under half of Leave voters had a negative view of multiculturalism, with one quarter having mixed feelings and the other quarter seeing it as positive. One third of BME voters opposed EU membership, including a majority of Sikhs and Jews. The political outlook of Leave voters was equally mixed. More than one third of Labour and SNP and a majority of Plaid Cymru supporters opted to leave the EU, along with a quarter of Greens and almost one third of Lib Dems. Almost half of voters (45%) described either capitalism, globalisation or both as overall a force for ill in society, the majority of them opposing EU membership. In fact, they comprised around one-third of anti-EU voters.[1] Moreover, as Susan Watkins (2016, p 23) pointed out, in the

> Leave districts that have been depressed since the 1970s, with GDP per capita less than half inner-London levels, and now hardest hit by cutbacks in services and benefits, bleakness and desperation appear to have trumped economic fear … Since the 1990s, their electoral protests have been all but invalidated by New Labour's ensconcement in the first-past-the-post system – Blair, Mandelson and the Milibands all assigned themselves safe seats in the North-East.

Contrary to popular belief, 52% of people who voted Leave lived in the southern half of England, and 59% were in the middle classes, while the proportion of Leave voters in the lowest two social classes was just 24%.[2]

Laying the basis for 'socialist decentralisation'

The British Parliament should be a federal institution elected by STV in multi-member constituencies, and have powers over currency, interest rates, banking, trade, foreign policy and defence. It should primarily be concerned with redistribution from rich to poor, across England,

Scotland and Wales (excluding Northern Ireland when Ireland is reunified on the basis of popular consent, North and South), the UK's regions and its localities based on social need. The special status enjoyed by capital in the Isle of Man and Channel Isles, which are run as semi-feudal big-business fiefdoms, should also be ended. Instead, the peoples of these islands should be democratically represented in the Westminster Parliament, with their own democratic parliaments – Tynwald and the States – and similar powers to Wales, Scotland and England's regions. Moreover, the House of Lords should be abolished and the Church of England should be disestablished.

Hence, this study concludes that laying the basis for 'socialist decentralisation' in a federal Britain and reinvigorating local government requires the following:

1. No to membership of the EU single market and TTIP/CETA; negotiation of new bilateral and multilateral agreements for mutually beneficial cooperation with European and other countries; rejection of European Court of Justice rulings protecting the super-exploitation of migrant workers; reversal of the unfair anti-immigration rules imposed on non-Europeans as part of the EU 'Fortress Europe' policy; enactment of progressive EU social and environmental policies into British law; continued funding of vital programmes previously supported via the EU; guaranteed residence for EU citizens currently living in the UK; and upholding the Human Rights Act and the European Convention on Human Rights (Chapter Five).

2. The reunification of Ireland on the basis of popular consent (Chapter Five).

3. Abolition of the House of Lords and disestablishment of the Church of England as the official state church (Chapter Five).

4. A directly elected Cornish Assembly to reflect the distinctive cultural and social characteristics of Cornwall with powers that match local aspirations (Chapter Two).

5. Representation of the Isle of Man and Channel Isles in the Westminster Parliament (Chapter Five).

6. Restoration of the democratic and civil liberties abolished or eroded by Conservative and Labour governments since 1979 (Chapters Three and Five).

7. The right to petition for a by-election to ensure that representatives are accountable (Chapters Two and Three).

8. No state funding for political parties; and corporate political donations to be submitted to a ballot of the employers and employees of the enterprise concerned (Chapter Five).

9. Setting the age of adulthood, including the right to vote, at 16 to reflect the other freedoms and responsibilities acquired by many young people at that age (Chapter Two).

10. The STV system for all elections (Chapters Two, Three and Five).

11. Abolition of the City of London Corporation, where non-residential business voters greatly exceed residential voters (Chapter Three).

12. Repeal of the Localism Act 2011, the Police Reform and Social Responsibility Act 2011, the Cities and Local Government Devolution Act 2016, the Housing and Planning Act 2016, the Education and Adoption Act 2016 and the Welfare Reform and Work Act 2016 (Chapters One, Two, Three, Four and Five).

13. An overall reorganisation of the structure and governance of local government in the UK to eliminate its democratic deficit compared with the rest of Europe. That is, there should be more councillors and councils, each with the committee system (which is much more inclusive than any other form of local governance such as the cabinet system with DEMs and gives all councillors the right to make policy again) and a police authority (made up of elected local councillors, representatives of trade unions and community organisations) covering smaller areas (Chapters One, Two and Three).

14. Mechanisms to enhance, strengthen and reform local democracy involving citizens with elected members in devising progressive policies with the wider community, small businesses and local charities (Chapters One, Two and Five).

15. No councillor to be paid more than the median gross weekly full-time earnings in their locality (Chapter One).

16. Restoration of the Standards Board to make criminal activity by councillors less – not more – likely (Chapter One).

17. Councils to be the default providers of services (Chapter One).

18. Termination of the PFI/PPP programme and replacement by direct public investment (Chapters One and Five).

19. Public consultation before any outsourcing of services or privatisation of assets takes place (Chapter One).

20. An in-house bid always to be on the table (or a reason given if there isn't) with social value the priority (Chapter One).

21. Private providers to be subject to freedom of information requests (Chapter One).

22. Public service contracts, performance and financial data to be publicly available (Chapter One).

23. The public to have the right to recall providers who do a bad job (Chapter One).

24. A new system of local government finance based on an annual LVT applied to all land to replace the council tax, the national non-domestic rates and stamp duty land tax (Chapter Four).

25. Support for the People's Assembly Manifesto for a fairer economy and fairer Britain; more and better jobs; high-standard homes for all (including a mass council house-building programme to build homes economically and quickly for all classes by direct labour with craft training for apprentices); improved public services; fairness and justice; and a secure and sustainable future (Chapter Five).

The current balance of political forces in the UK

The 2014 local elections in Northern Ireland

Elections were held to 462 seats in 11 local authorities in Northern Ireland on 22 May 2014. These were the first elections to take place following the implementation of reforms to local government administration, with the number of local authorities reduced from

26 to 11. These new councils operated in shadow form until they assumed full responsibilities in 2015. During this period they approved business and financial plans, set rates for 2015/16, appointed senior staff and led cooperation between merging councils in preparation for taking on full powers and responsibilities. Councillors are elected under a system of STV. The share of seats held by each party remains broadly consistent with that won in the last elections in 2011. The Democratic Unionist Party (DUP) won 130 seats, representing 28% of the total contested seats, down from a 30% share of seats in the 2011 local elections. Sinn Fein secured 105 seats, 23% of those contested and a slight reduction on the 24% of seats won in 2011. The Ulster Unionist Party increased its share of seats from 18% to 19%, while the Social Democratic and Labour Party and Alliance parties both lost around half a percentage point of their share of seats as compared to 2011 (House of Commons Library, 2014, p 13).

The UK general election, May 2015

The Conservatives won 51% of the seats in the general election on 7 May 2015, with 37% of the votes cast by only 24% of the electorate, and a majority of 12 seats – which few had predicted, due to the decline of the two-party system.[3] The result of the election was decided in a handful of 'marginal' swing seats and was also the most disproportionate result in British history: since on average it took 23,000 votes to elect a DUP MP, 26,000 votes to elect an SNP MP, 34,000 to elect a Conservative MP, 40,000 to elect a Labour MP, 291,000 to elect a Liberal Democrat MP, 1.1 million to elect the only Green MP and 3.8 million to elect the only UKIP MP. The SNP won around 1.5 million votes and 56 seats, while the DUP got fewer than 200,000 votes yet the same number of MPs as the 2.5 million vote-strong Lib Dems. Moreover, as the Electoral Reform Society (ERS) noted, out of the almost 31 million people who voted, 15.4 million voted for losing candidates. And many of the MPs who did win failed to get the support of most voters. Out of 650 winning candidates, 321 (49%) got less than 50% of the vote; and 191 MPs were elected with the support of less than 30% of their whole electorate (Garland and Terry, 2015, pp 21–3).

How, then, would it be different under a fair voting system? The ERS's preferred method is the STV system, which preserves the local link in multi-member constituencies and is already used for local government elections in Northern Ireland and Scotland. Under STV in 2015 the Conservatives would have got 276 seats instead of 331; Labour 236 instead of 232; the Lib Dems 26 seats instead of 8; UKIP, which is attracting a significant chunk of Labour's former working-class electorate, 54 seats instead of 1; the Greens 3 seats instead of 1; and the SNP 34 seats instead of 56. Labour increased its share of the UK vote by 1.5% as compared to the 2010 general election – that is, by more than the Tories, whose share increased by only 0.8%, but less than the increase of 3.1% for the SNP and 2.8% for the Greens. Although the Tories won 331 seats and Labour won only 232 seats, Labour increased its vote by 737,799 compared to 2010, whereas the Tories increased their vote by only 607,962. Left-wing parties gained 2,563,382 votes and right-wing parties lost 1,466,124 votes. Furthermore, in 11 marginals that Labour lost to the Tories, the Green vote was bigger than the Tory candidate's majority. In another eight seats, the numbers of votes for the Greens and other anti-austerity parties – such as Plaid Cymru or the Trade Unionist and Socialist Coalition (which had 135 candidates and got 36,327 votes) – were more than Labour lost by. Therefore, if Labour had won 12 of these seats, it would have been enough to deny the Tories a majority.[4]

The 2015 local elections in England

Elections were held in 279 English local authorities on 7 May 2015 (36 metropolitan boroughs, 194 of the second-tier districts and 49 of the unitary authorities). The Conservatives had net gains of 541 seats and 32 local councils (mostly with no overall control before the elections). They retained control of Solihull and Trafford, the only two metropolitan boroughs that they had held before the elections, slightly increasing their majority on both. Among the unitary councils, the Conservatives won control of Bath and North East Somerset for the first time. Labour had net losses of 203 seats and lost control of Walsall metropolitan borough and the Plymouth and Stoke-on-Trent unitary authorities (both to no overall control). The Lib Dems had net losses of 411 seats and lost control of three district councils (Hinckley & Bosworth, South Somerset and Three Rivers) and one borough council (Watford). The Green Party had a net gain of 10 seats but lost control of Brighton and Hove City Council (the first and only council in which it had been the largest party) to Labour. UKIP won control of Thanet District Council, going from 2 to 33 seats – the first time that it had won control of a local council.[5]

The net fall in the number of councils with no overall control was 51. Moreover, according to an analysis by Colin Rallings and Michael Thrasher, three-quarters of councils across the UK are now under the majority control of the two largest parties, Conservative and Labour – the highest percentage since the 1970s local government reform. The two main parties also held 77% of seats, the highest since 1980. The decline of the Lib Dems accounted for part of this trend. Rallings and Thrasher therefore concluded 'that much is said about multi-party UK but it is time instead to talk about two-party local government' (*Local Government Chronicle*, 11 May, 2015).

The 2016 local elections in England

Elections were held for 2,782 seats on 124 local councils in England on 5 May 2016. These elections comprised 1,393 seats on 70 district councils; 468 seats on 19 unitary authority councils; and 921 seats on 35 metropolitan borough councils.

Labour's national equivalent vote share in the local elections of 2016 returned to being above the Conservatives' after having fallen in 2015. Labour had 33%, as compared to 30% in 2015, while the Conservatives had 32%, as compared to 37% in 2015. The Lib Dems increased their vote share for the first time since 2009 by increasing from 8% in 2015 to 14% in 2016. This was their highest national equivalent vote share since 2012 (15%). The 'other parties' category fell in 2016 to 21%, from 25% in 2015. Included in this category, UKIP fell to 12% in 2016 from a high of 22% in 2013 (House of Commons Library, 2016a, p 15).

Labour won or retained 1,319 of the 2,782 council seats up for election in May 2016 (47% of the total seats up for election). The Conservatives won or retained 851 seats (31% of the total seats up for election) and the Lib Dems 377 (14%). UKIP won or retained 62 seats and the Green Party 49 seats. The Conservatives made a net loss of 38 seats, the most of any party. Labour made a net loss of 15, while the Lib Dems made a net gain of 48. Comparing the May 2016 situation to that of May 2015, across all council seats in England the Conservatives made a net loss of 51, Labour a net loss of 11 and the Lib Dems a net gain of 41 (House of Commons Library, 2016a, pp 13–14).

The Conservatives won or retained 38 of the councils that had elections on 5 May 2016, and now control a total of 191 councils overall. This is a net change of 2 on the composition following the 2015 elections. Elmbridge Council was all up in May 2016 and the Conservatives lost control to no overall control (NOC) after losing 11 councillors, leaving them with 22. It is important to note, however, that due to boundary changes, the council was reduced from 60 seats to 48. The Conservatives also lost Worcester to NOC but they did gain Peterborough from NOC. The Labour Party won or retained control of 58 councils and now controls a total of 114 councils. This is a net change of +1 on the composition following the 2015 elections. In Bristol Labour took the council from NOC after winning 7 extra seats, leaving it with 37 out of a possible 70 councillors. It lost Dudley to NOC after losing 3 councillors. The Lib Dems gained Watford Council, and increased their number of councillors by 7, giving them 25 out of a possible 36. They won or retained control of four councils, which leaves them in control of seven councils, a net change of +1 on the composition following the 2015 elections. Following defections in October 2015, UKIP does not now control Thanet, which has returned to NOC (House of Commons Library, 2016a, p 12).

As shown in Chapter Two, out of the 16 local authority DEMs in England 12 are Labour and only one is a Conservative (Torbay). The Conservatives control no councils in Wales, where 10 out of 22 are controlled by Labour, three are controlled by independents and nine have no overall control, and Scotland, where five out of 32 are controlled by Labour, two are controlled by the SNP, two are controlled by independents and 23 have NOC (Edkins, 2016). Nevertheless, the Tories are still hegemonic with 8,709 councillors (43%), which is 57 less than the 8,766 they had in May 2015, and control 191 councils (47%) – one less of the three nations' 405 councils after the May 2015 local elections. Labour has 6,851 councillors (34%), which is 22 less than the 6,873 it had in May 2015, and controls 115 councils (28%) – one more than in May 2015. The Lib Dems have 1,822 councillors (9%), which is 12 more than they had in May 2015, and control seven councils (2%) – one more than in May 2015. The SNP has 418 councillors and controls two councils. Plaid Cymru has 171 councillors and does not control any councils. There are a further 2,251 councillors (11%) who are either independents or members of other parties (House of Commons Library, 2015b, pp 13 and 15; 2016a, pp 18–19).

The Greater London mayoral and Assembly elections, 5 May 2016

Elections for the London Mayor and London Assembly were held on 5 May 2016. The Labour Party candidate, Sadiq Khan, won 1,148,716 first preference votes (44.2%), compared to 909,755 for Conservative Party candidate Zac Goldsmith (35.0%). The total number of votes cast for Khan rose to 1,310,143 after second preference votes were redistributed, ahead of Goldsmith with 994,614 votes. Khan won the highest number and share of first preference votes since mayoral elections began in 2000 (House of Commons Library, 2016b, p 3).

The Green Party's candidate, Sian Berry, came third with 150,673 first preference votes. Caroline Pidgeon of the Lib Dems finished fourth with 120,005 first preference votes. Labour won 12 of the 25 seats in the London Assembly elections, the same number as in 2012, and remains the largest party in the Assembly. It won 43.5% of the Assembly constituency votes, a 1.3% increase on 2012. Labour's vote share in the mayoral election increased by 3.9%. The Conservatives have eight seats, one fewer than in 2012. The Green Party and UKIP both have two seats, and the Lib Dems, who lost one seat, now hold one Assembly seat (House of Commons Library, 2016b, p 3).

The Welsh Assembly elections, 5 May 2016

The system for electing members to the Welsh National Assembly and the Scottish Assembly is known as the Additional Member System. Voters are given two ballot papers. The first is used to elect each of the constituency members under the traditional first-past-the-post system. The second is used to elect members from each of the electoral regions. These additional members are elected so that the total representation from each geographical area, including those members elected under first-past-the-post, corresponds more closely to the share of the votes cast for each political party in the region.

Labour fell short of a majority, winning 29 of the 60 seats in the Welsh National Assembly. The seats won by each party were as follows: Conservatives 11, Labour 29, Lib Dems 1, Plaid Cymru 12 and UKIP 7. Labour's share of the vote fell to 33.2%, from 39.6% in 2011, but it remained the largest party in the National Assembly. Plaid Cymru overtook the Conservatives as the second-largest party with 20.7%, up from 18.6%. The Conservatives polled 20.0%, 3.8% points less than in 2011. UKIP's share rose by 10.4% points to 12.7%, compared to 2.3% in 2011. The Lib Dem share fell to 7.1% from 9.3%, and the Green Party polled 2.7%, up from 1.8%. Average turnout across all the constituencies and regions was 45.4%, up by 4.0% from 2011. The highest turnout was in Cardiff North (56.8%) and Brecon & Radnorshire (56.5%). The lowest turnout was in Alyn & Deeside (34.6%). Following the elections, the Assembly comprises 35 men and 25 women. The number of women Assembly Members has increased by one, compared to 2011. It is three fewer than in 2007 and five fewer than in the 2003, when equal numbers of men and women were elected. There are currently two BME Assembly Members (House of Commons Library, 2016c, pp 5 and 7).

The Scottish Parliament elections, 5 May 2016

In the elections to the Scottish Parliament in May 2016 the SNP won the most seats (63 out of 129) with 44.1% of the votes, but failed to win an overall majority. The total number of SNP MSPs elected was six fewer than in 2011. The Conservatives came second with 31 seats and 22.5% of the vote. The number of Conservative MSPs more than doubled, and their share of the vote increased by 9.4%. This was the best performance for the Conservatives at any Scottish Parliament election so far. Labour came third with 24 seats and 20.8% of the vote. Labour lost 13 seats and its share of the vote fell by 8.2%. The Lib Dems won five seats and 6.5% of the vote, while the Scottish Green Party won six seats and 3.6% of the vote. Average turnout across all constituencies and regions increased from 50.4% in 2011 to 55.7% in 2016. The highest constituency turnout was in Eastwood, where 68.3% of the electorate cast valid ballots. The lowest constituency turnout was in Glasgow Provan, where 42.9% of eligible voters participated. Following the elections, the composition of the Scottish Parliament is 84 men and 45 women. The number of women MSPs is the same as in the 2011 elections and two more than in the 2007 elections. Two BME MSPs were elected, which was the same number as in the 2011 Parliament. Both are men (House of Commons Library, 2016d, pp 3 and 5–6).

The crisis of working-class political representation and ways in which it is now beginning to be addressed

The lukewarm Left's refusal to confront structures of inequality

Failure to radically redistribute wealth and income at the same time as 'the inequality gap is growing', as the French economist Thomas Piketty told Andrew Hussey, will 'mean for ordinary people ... the degradation of the public sector' (quoted in the *Observer*, 13 April 2014). Piketty also shows that from 1945 to 1975 the reduction in private-wealth levels led to the illusion that we had entered a new phase of capitalism – a kind of capitalism without capital, or at least without capital*ists*. But capitalism had not been superseded in any structural way; instead this was essentially a transitional phase of reconstruction. Wealth was restored, albeit gradually. It's only today, in the early 21st century, that we find the same levels of wealth as in the years leading up to the First World War: around six times annual national income, as opposed to little more than twice national income in the 1950s. (Piketty, 2014a, pp 104–5, his emphasis)

Therefore Piketty proposes a top tax rate of 82% in advanced capitalist countries on annual incomes above $500,000 a year; and a flat tax of 15% on private wealth, which he admits is 'utopian' (Piketty, 2014b) – for, as Paul Mason comments, it is 'easier to imagine capitalism collapsing than the elite consenting to such taxes'. Nevertheless, as Mason (*Guardian*, 29 April 2014) also notes, Piketty

> challenges the narrative of the centre-left under globalisation, which believed upskilling the workforce, combined with mild redistribution, would promote social justice. This, Piketty demonstrates, is mistaken. All that social democracy and liberalism can produce, with their current policies, is the oligarch's yacht co-existing with the foodbank for ever.

The result is that many of the current generation of young people are likely to be the first to occupy a lower occupational and class position than their parents, in spite of being better qualified. Beneath them, a section of the traditional working class has expanded into a new underclass – Marx's 'reserve army of labour' – in 'permanent precarity' (Ainley, 2016, p 60).

Moreover, as John Arlige points out:

the UK's super-rich have powered through the economic
crisis and are now more than twice as rich as in 2009 when
the economy was on the rocks … Today the wealthiest
1,000 people based in the UK are collectively worth
£547 billion, up from £258 billion in 2009, an increase
of 112% … There are now 117 sterling billionaires based
in the UK, up 12% on last year and up 172% on 2009.
That is … more per head of population than in any other
country in the G20 group of the world's richest nations
… London boasts more billionaires than … any other city
– 80. The capital's nearest European rival, Paris, has one
quarter of that figure … (*Sunday Times*, 26 April 2015)

And though the declining fortunes of some of the UK's wealthiest
people – such as Lakshmi Mittal, whose steel company lost £5.5 billion
in 2015 – contributed to the first levelling-off of wealth among the
top 0.001% for six years, they were still worth £343.943 billion in
2016, up 5.79% on the £325.131 billion in 2015 (*Sunday Times*, 24
April 2016).

In addition, between 2011 and 2015, 197 people contributed
£82.4 million to political parties – just under half of the £147 million
donated in private and corporate cash. The Tories received more than
three-quarters of the £82.4 million from 151 of the 197 donors. Thus,
as Alistair McCall et al concluded, the 'bankrolling of British politics
is increasingly concentrated in the hands of an already privileged
few' (*Sunday Times*, 19 April 2015). Therefore, there should be no
state funding for political parties, so that they have to rely largely on
voluntary donations from the people they claim to represent; and
corporate political donations should be submitted to a ballot of the
employers and employees of the enterprise concerned.

The following further developments, however, indicate that the
crisis of social democracy and working-class political representation
– albeit far from being resolved – is now beginning to be addressed.

The alternative economic and political strategy (AEPS)

Over two decades the unions, individually and at the TUC, have abandoned the policy planks that bound them into capitalist consensus. For example, the 2011 TUC adopted an Alternative Economic Strategy and voted for an LVT; the 2012 TUC voted for public ownership of the banks, reiterated its support for re-nationalisation of the railways and reaffirmed its support for the People's Charter and the Women's Charter; and the 2016 TUC supported a universal basic income paid individually, alongside comprehensive public services and childcare.[6] This is significant because unions are by far the most inclusive, representative and deeply rooted popular organisations in Britain. Combine the settled views of millions of trade unionists and workers generally (including big sections of middle strata opinion), and we have the popular basis of a genuinely alternative government programme arising from real lived experiences. Hence there is vital work to do to persuade people across Britain that austerity is unnecessary.

Labour's national leadership until the election of Jeremy Corbyn as leader was committed to neoliberalism, austerity and 'corporate welfare' – that is, all the subsidies and grants paid to business, as well as the corporate tax loopholes, subsidised credit, export guarantees, which came to £93 billion and amounted to £3,500 a year from each UK household (*Guardian*, 8 July 2015). This was greater than the entire public sector deficit in 2015/16 (excluding the effects of the bank bailout) of £89.2 billion. And, as Michael Burke argues, 'It is business, not the poor, people with disabilities, women burdened by increased carer responsibilities or public sector workers who should shoulder the burden of the crisis they created' (Burke, 2015). Therefore, to fund increased provision of directly provided local authority and other public services, the threshold for income tax should be raised to £20,000 per annum and, in stages, later to £30,000, retaining the basic rate of tax at 20%; and a new 60% rate of tax for incomes over £60,000 should be introduced. In addition, the estimated revenue from

- a 2% annual wealth tax on the richest 10% of the population (who owned 45% of Great Britain's wealth in 2012/14, estimated to be £11.1 trillion) would be £100 billion a year;[7]
- ending tax dodging by the super-rich and big business would be £120 billion a year;[8]
- a 'Robin Hood' tax on City transactions would be £7.5 billion to £112 billion a year (McCulloch and Pacillo, 2011).

The People's Assembly Against Austerity

The People's Assembly Against Austerity was launched in a letter to the *Guardian* on 5 February 2013. Signatories included Tony Benn, Bob Crow of the RMT and eight other union general secretaries; the National Union of Students; four MPs (Caroline Lucas, Katy Clark, Jeremy Corbyn and John McDonnell); the Communist Party of Britain, the *Morning Star*, Socialist Resistance, the New Economics Foundation, CND, Stop the War Coalition, the National Association of Women, Keep our NHS Public, Disabled People Against the Cuts, the Indian Workers Association, Black activists rising against the cuts, the National Unemployed Workers Centres Combine, the Institute of Employment Rights, War on Want, authors, journalists and actors. Additional supporters now include the TUC, the Anti-Academies alliance, the Campaign Against Climate Change, the Campaign for Trade Union Freedom, the Fire Brigades Union, Left Unity, the Muslim Council of Britain, the National Pensioners Convention and the University and College Union.

The Assembly also now has 86 local groups in England, Scotland and Wales – 32 of which were formed after hundreds of thousands marched against the chancellor's class-war Budget on 20 June 2015.[9] The Norfolk People's Assembly has 'united thousands of activists and campaigners with ordinary people, many of whom have never been involved in this kind of "politics" before'. They are led by women; most officers are women and the majority at their meetings are women. The trade unions fund them. And when Norwich City Council threatened to evict families for bedroom tax arrears they extracted a public promise from the deputy leader that no tenant would be evicted (*Morning Star*, 15 March 2014).

Antonio Gramsci referred to three phases of political development that *any* class must pass through. 'Economic corporate' refers to self-interest (for example, joining a trade union due to fear of cuts). In the second phase a sense of solidarity develops based on shared economic interests. But it is only by passing through the third phase that hegemony really becomes possible as members become aware that their interests need to be extended beyond what they can do within the context of their own particular class (see Latham, 2011a, pp 29–30). Therefore rigorous work on the ground is now needed in local communities to win support for the AEPS.

Jeremy Corbyn – twice elected Labour Party leader

Jeremy Corbyn has been Leader of the Labour Party since 12 September 2015. This was the first Labour leadership contest to be fought under the new 'one member one vote' system designed to reduce the influence of affiliated trade union members. There was also a new category of registered supporters, who paid £3 to join. In both the leadership and deputy-leadership contests, according to Labour's website, 343,995 votes (81.3%) were cast online, which was the UK's largest online ballot. Turnout for the leadership vote was 422,871 (76.3%) of the 554,272 eligible voters, with 207 spoilt ballots. Turnout among the three categories ranged from 48.5% for affiliated trade union supporters to 83.5% for members and, highest of all, 93% for registered voters. Jeremy Corbyn received 59.5% of the valid votes cast and was way ahead of his rivals among all three categories of voters. He received half of the full members' votes; 58% of the affiliated trade union members' votes; and a massive 84% of the registered supporters' votes. His policies during the election campaign included: an end to austerity, people's quantitative easing, a national investment bank, higher taxes on the rich and big business, public ownership of the railways, Royal Mail and energy utilities, more council housing, rent controls, breaking up the media monopolies, the abolition of Trident and withdrawal from NATO.

Nor was Corbyn's triumph in the leadership contest only a personal one, or one for his supporters. It was a victory for popular protest and mass mobilisation – the very things that we are constantly told are 'out of date', marginal or futile. Many of the 251,000 people who first elected Corbyn were drawn into political activity through their opposition to austerity, privatisation, the bedroom tax and the Iraq War. They comprised most of the 100,000 and more new Labour Party members and registered supporters who voted for the candidate closely associated with the People's Assembly, CND and the Stop the War Coalition. Yet the Commons voted for Trident renewal by a majority of 355 on 18 July 2016. In total, 140 Labour MPs voted in favour of the motion and 47 against, with 40 absent and one abstention. Hence the Tories' plan to divert at least £205 billion away from socially useful programmes may spark the biggest revival of CND and the peace movement since the anti-cruise missile struggle of the 1980s. Unions in the arms industry have a critical role to play – to show how their members' skills and associated technology can produce valuable non-military goods instead of nuclear weapons. For example, the Scottish TUC and Scottish CND have shown how the Barrow and Clyde shipyards could be used to build ultra-fuel-efficient freight ships and deep-water oil-exploration vessels (STUC, 2015).

Since 2015 there has been an upsurge of trade union strikes and demonstrations. Thus, extra-parliamentary campaigning and industrial action can combine with parliamentary and inner-party struggle to change the whole political situation. Furthermore, Labour Party membership has massively increased and moved to the left: a week after the 2015 general election party membership stood at 221,247. By July 2016 it had more than doubled to 515,00, while the Conservative Party had 149,800 members; the SNP had around 120,000; the Liberal Democrat Party had 76,000; the Green Party (England and Wales) had 55,500 ; UKIP had around 39,000; and Plaid Cymru had 8,273 (House of Commons Library, 2016g, p 3). But there is still a crisis of working-class representation in local councils. For example, only six out of Croydon's 40 Labour councillors attended Jeremy Corbyn's meeting in the town on 4 August 2015, because, as Paul Mason notes, most Labour councillors 'would rather he did not exist' (*Guardian*, 22 December 2015). Moreover, as the Labour Representation Committee (2014) notes: 'Some Labour councillors appear to need reminding that they are political representatives and not just competent and compassionate administrators.' Hence, if Labour fails to respond to the challenge of building a mass campaign of resistance to Tory-driven austerity at local level, it will fail to create the political basis in public opinion for getting a radical Corbyn-led Labour government elected.

Those MPs plotting to overthrow Corbyn used the EU referendum result as an excuse to spark a leadership contest that paralysed the party for months. The turnout in 2016 was 77.4% – up from 76.3% in 2015; and most Labour MPs and councillors voted for the other candidate, Owen Smith. Corbyn's mandate increased from 59.5% in 2015 to 61.8% in 2016, and would have been even higher if thousands of members had not been barred from voting. For example, in August 2016 Labour's NEC won its bid to overturn a High Court decision allowing 130,000 new members to vote who had joined less than six months previously (*Guardian*, 13 August 2016). During the contest 3,107 people were suspended from the party – the overwhelming majority of whom were Corbyn supporters, including three councillors in Bristol, which resulted in Labour losing control of the council (*Morning Star*, 22 September 2016). Yet Corbyn still won support from 57% of party members, 70% of registered supporters and 60% of affiliated supporters – the first time he had won a majority in all three categories. But the 2016 Labour Party Conference voted to allow one full member of the NEC each to be nominated by the Scottish Labour leader, Kezia Dugdale, and the Welsh first minister, Carwyn Jones (who have both been critical of Corbyn) rather than being chosen by members. Hence Corbyn's allies lost their majority on the NEC, despite six left-wing candidates being elected to the executive prior to the conference (*Guardian*, 28 September 2016). However, Corbyn wrested back control of the NEC when he removed shadow health secretary Jonathan Ashworth, who is not seen as an ally, from his role on the NEC and replaced him with the supportive Kate Osamor (*Guardian*, 8 October 2016).

Theresa May, when she gave the now-traditional One-Nation Tory Party-of-the-Workers nod to the unwashed on her coronation, said: "The government I lead will not be driven by the interests of the privileged few." However, although chancellor Philip Hammond said at the Tory Party's 2016 conference that he had ditched predecessor George Osborne's promise to attain a budget surplus by 2019/20 and claimed to be ready to invest in infrastructure and skills to raise productivity, when speaking in Washington on 7 October 2016 he said that the previously announced 're-set' to fiscal policy would be on a modest scale (quoted in the *Guardian*, 8 October 2016). The Tories' £5 billion homeownership plans also ignore council housing, on the bizarre grounds that it increases inequality. And Work and Pensions Secretary Damian Green told the BBC's *Andrew Marr Show* on 18 September 2016 that: "We will meet the previous commitments we've made." But despite his promise of "different language" about benefit claimants, he refused to consider rowing back on cruel policies such as benefit sanctions and fitness-for-work tests – the subject of Ken Loach's film, *I, Daniel Blake*.

Moreover, George Osborne had promised £300 million of 'transition' funding for increasingly inadequate social care budgets. But so far the top 10 beneficiaries of this new money run as follows: Surrey, Hampshire, Hertfordshire, Essex, West Sussex, Kent, Buckinghamshire, Oxfordshire, Leicestershire and Cambridgeshire. Eight of these councils have an outright Conservative majority, and all are Tory run. Heading up the list of councils that have not received a penny are those that run Nottingham, Birmingham, Bristol, Leeds, Liverpool, Manchester, Newcastle and Sheffield. All have a Labour majority. The government says that the new funds are being handed out in 'direct proportion' to particular councils' reductions in support due to changes in the way money is distributed from Whitehall; but it will not – according to the *Guardian*, 23 September 2016 – release figures to back up that claim. In addition, although Employment Support Allowance (ESA) claimants suffering from life-long, chronic illnesses

will no longer be required to attend repeated 'fitness for work' tests
to prove their eligibility for sickness benefits, ministers have reiterated
their intention to cut payments for claimants in the ESA 'Work Related
Activity' group by £30 a week from April 2017, reducing payments
to a level similar to Jobseeker's Allowance (*Welfare Weekly*, 1 October
2016). Moreover, as the Labour Land Campaign's press release noted,
the Autumn Statement 2016's

> subsidies for builders, transport infrastructure and Business
> Rates will immediately capitalise into land value, thereby
> further the enriching the wealthy ... If Philip Hammond
> were serious about making the economy work for
> everyone, the underlying causes of low productivity, the
> housing crisis and growing inequality would have been
> 'tackled' ... But then, his party has powerful vested interests
> to keep happy (the wealthy and specifically landowners).

A left-led Labour Party on a left-wing programme could win the next
general election, which would inspire millions more people to register
and vote, especially among the young, unemployed, students, housing
tenants and the ethnic minorities, where electoral turnout is low. In
2015, Labour received two million fewer votes than the Tories. Yet
15 million electors didn't vote on that occasion, nor did 13 million
in the EU referendum. Millions of these people could be won for
a bold alternative to Tory austerity, privatisation, poor housing and
poverty. However, the new electoral boundary proposals will slash the
number of MPs from 650 to 600 when the population is growing,
and the Tories are packing the unelected House of Lords with their
supporters. The proposed new seats are not based on how many people
live in them, but on December 2015's electoral register. A new system
of individual registration also means that hundreds of thousands of
people were wiped from the register. Disproportionately, they tended
to be young, private tenants and from BME backgrounds. Because
of the referendum effect, another two million people have joined
the electoral register since, but the new seats do not take them into

account. Indeed, according to Labour's Jonathan Ashworth, the new Lewisham constituencies will be based on an electoral register that is missing 20% of voters (*Guardian*, 14 September 2016). Combined with other assaults on democracy – from legislation to cripple trade unions to a so-called 'gagging bill' that intends to silence non-governmental organisations – the picture is clear: even when Labour is in a position to effectively challenge the Conservatives, everything will be stacked in favour of the ruling party. Hence, alliances on the left will still be crucial to beating the Tories (see Nandy et al, 2016).

Nor are Labour's internal divisions going to be solved by Corbyn's second victory, which will require turning a mass membership into a mass movement for change. Thus, as Hilary Wainwright argues, the Labour Party leadership needs to engage in a process of empowering education among its members and supporters, the labour movement and its allies. Several of Corbyn's initiatives indicate his openness to this kind of process: for example, popular participation in the drawing up of Labour's manifesto and the national day of action to campaign for 'inclusive education' on 1 October 2016. And there also many other initiatives that are not only resisting austerity but also involving people in developing alternatives: for example, the National Union of Teachers reaching out to parents and the wider community. Furthermore:

> the separation of MPs from the people, and the crisis over Corbyn's leadership, makes the issue of democratising the British state an urgent issue for the grassroots membership of the Labour Party as well as the broader left ... It is exactly this that the establishment fear most from the dynamics unleashed by Corbyn's leadership: that is, the democratic potential to realise a transformative politics beyond 'parliamentary socialism'. (Wainwright, 2016, p 100)

Finally, as Whyeda Gill-McLure (2014, p 388) observes, the term 'Modernisation' has been hijacked and made a synonym for 'privatisation'. Municipal unions argued over a century ago that modernisation should mean direct labour managed, not through the profit and patronage motive, but through the principles of public service devoted to public need.

Therefore this study, as Gill–McLure also emphasises, 'points to an urgent need to *re-modernise* along these lines'.

Notes

[1] http://lordashcroftpolls.com/wp-content/uploads/2016/06/How-the-UK-voted-Full-tables-1.pdf

[2] http://www.dannydorling.org/?p=5568

[3] http://www.bbc.co.uk/news/election/2015/results

[4] http://www.bbc.co.uk/news/election/2015/results

[5] http://www.bbc.co.uk/news/election/2015/results/councils

[6] http://www.tuc.org.uk

[7] https://www.ons.gov.uk/peoplepopulationandcommunity/personalandhouseholdfinances/incomeandwealth/compendium/wealthingreatbritainwave4/2012to2014

[8] http://www.taxresearch.org.uk/Documents/FAQ1TaxGap.pdf

[9] http://www.thepeoplesassembly.org.uk/local-groups

REFERENCES

Adam, S., Johnson, P. and Roantree, B. (2013) *Taxing an independent Scotland*, Briefing Note 141, October, London: IFS.

Ainley, P. (2016) *Betraying a generation: How education is failing young people*, Bristol: Policy Press.

APSE (Association for Public Service Excellence) (2015) *Two tribes? Exploring the future role of elected members*, Manchester: APSE.

Association of Greater Manchester Authorities, NHS England, NHS Greater Manchester Association of Clinical Commissioning Groups (2015) *Greater Manchester Health and Social Care Devolution Memorandum of Understanding*.

Bentley, G. (2012) 'The Localism Act: the implications for local economic development and Local Enterprise Partnerships', in *The world will be your oyster?*, Birmingham: INLOGOV, pp 73–80.

BATC (Birmingham Against the Cuts) (2016) 'The West Midlands Combined Authority – what it is and what it should be. For a People's Plan for the WMCA', July.

Burke, M. (2015) 'Economic failure, austerity continues', *Socialist Economic Bulletin*, 18 March.

Burt, P., Baillie, J., Daniels, P. and Lowe, J. (2006) *A fairer way: Report by the Local Government Finance Review Committee*, November, Edinburgh: Local Government Finance Review Committee.

Carr-West, J. (2013) 'Is local government heading for broke?', 8 October, http://blogs.lse.ac.uk/politicsandpolicy/archives/36972.

Centre for Local Economic Strategies (2014) *Austerity uncovered*, December, Manchester: CLES.

CfPS (Centre for Public Scrutiny) (2012) *Musical chairs: Practical issues for local authorities in moving to a committee system*, London: CfPS.

Chakrabarti, S. (2012) 'Policing, civil liberties and the rule of law', in R. Jethwa (ed) *Upholding the Queen's Peace: Towards a new consensus on policing*, Leatherhead, Surrey: Police Federation of England and Wales.

Cooper, C., Danson, M. and Whittam, G. (2010) 'The neoliberal project – local taxation intervention in Scotland', *Critical Perspectives on Accounting*, vol 21, pp 195–210.

Cooper, C., Danson, M. and Whittam, G. (2013) *Local taxation, spending and poverty: New choices and tax justice*, Poverty Alliance Discussion Paper, February, Glasgow: Poverty Alliance.

Copley, T. (2015) *Out of stock Right-to-Buy, HRA reform – the future of London's council housing stock*, London: Greater London Authority London Assembly Labour Group.

Copley, T. (2016) *Tax trial: A Land Value Tax for London?*, GLA (February), London: Greater London Authority.

Coulson, A. (2012) 'Go back to committees – and use all the talent of elected councillors', http://inlogov.wordpress.com/2012/05/02/committees-talent-councillors/.

CPB (Communist Party of Britain) (2014) *From each according to their means: A discussion pamphlet on essential tax reforms for a Left progressive programme*, December, Croydon: CPB.

Davies, J.S. (2011) *Challenging governance theory: From networks to hegemony*, Bristol: Policy Press.

Davies, S. (2011) *Mutual benefit? Should mutuals, co-operatives and social enterprises deliver public services?* London: Unison.

Defty, A. (2016) 'Improvements in turnout and more partisan voting: PCC elections 2016', http://blogs.lse.ac.uk/politicsandpolicy/improvements-in-turnout-and-more-partisan-voting-pcc-elections-2016/.

DCLG (Department for Communities and Local Government) (2011) *Localism Bill: Giving councils greater freedom over their governance arrangements impact assessment*, London: DCLG.

DCLG (2012) *The Housing Revenue Account self-financing determinations*, February, London: DCLG.

DCLG (2013) *Financial sustainability of local authorities*, January, London: DCLG.

DCLG (2016) *Local Government Financial Statistics England*, No 26, July, London: DCLG.

Dorling, D. (2014) *All that is solid: The great housing disaster*, London: Allen Lane.

Downey, A., Kirby, P. and Sherlock, N. (2010) *Payment for success – how to shift power from Whitehall to public service customers*, London: KPMG.

Edkins, K. (2016) 'Local council political compositions', 16 May, http://www.gwydir.demon.co.uk/uklocalgov/makeup.htm.

Electoral Commission (2011) *Referendum on the voting system for UK parliamentary elections: Report on the May 2011 referendum*, London: Electoral Commission.

Electoral Commission (2013) *Police and Crime Commissioner elections in England and Wales: Report on the administration of the elections held on 15 November 2012*, London: Electoral Commission.

Ertürk, I., Froud, J., Johal, S., Leaver, A., Moran, M., Williams, K. (2011) *City state against national settlement: UK economic policy and politics after the financial crisis*, CRESC Working Paper Series, Working Paper No 101, June, pp 1–43.

Foster, J. (2011) *The European Union: For the monopolies, against the people*, 2nd edn, March, Croydon: Communist Party of Britain.

Foster, J. (2016) *Britain and the EU: What next?*, February, Croydon: Communist Party of Britain.

FAI (Fraser of Allander Institute) (2016) *Scotland's Budget – 2016*, University of Strathclyde Business School, September.

Garland, J. and Terry, C. (2012) *How not to run an election. The Police and Crime Commissioner elections*, London: Electoral Reform Society.

Garland, J. and Terry, C. (2015) *The 2015 general election: A voting system in crisis*, London: Electoral Reform Society.

Gill-McLure, W. (2014) 'The politics of managerial reform in UK local government: a study of control, conflict and resistance 1880s to present', *Labor History*, vol 55, no 3, pp 365–88.

Hambleton, R. (2014) *Leading the inclusive city: Place-based innovation for a bounded planet*, Bristol: Policy Press.

Hambleton, R. (2016) 'Place-based leadership – new possibilities?', *Chartist*, July/August, pp 12–13.

Hatcher, R. (2011) '"Open Public Services" White Paper: the risky road to privatisation', 6 August, http://socialistresistance.org/2367/open-public-services-white-paper-the-risky-road-to-privatisation.

Hatcher, R. (2015a) 'The neoliberalisation of the city: the transformation of city centres and city councils', draft article, March.

Hatcher, R. (2015b) 'Some notes on combined authorities and implications for the forthcoming West Midlands Combined Authority', 30 March.

Hatcher, R. (2015c) 'Why does the government want combined authorities? And why does it want them run by directly elected mayors?', 11 June, http://socialistresistance.org/7508/why-does-the-government-want-combined-authorities.

Hatherley, O. (2010) *A guide to the new ruins of Great Britain*, London: Verso.

Hilary, J. (2014) *The Transatlantic Trade and Investment Partnership: A charter for deregulation, an attack on jobs, an end to democracy*, 2nd edn, September, London: War on Want.

HM Government (2011) *Open Public Services*, White Paper, July.

HM Government (2012) *Open Public Services*, March.

HM Government (2015) *Enabling closer working between the Emergency Services*, September.

HM Treasury (2015) *Spending Review and Autumn Statement 2015*, Cm 9162, November.

HM Treasury (2016a) *Private Finance Initiative and Private Finance 2 projects: 2015 summary data*, March.

HM Treasury (2016b) *Public Expenditure Statistical Analyses 2016*, July.

HM Treasury (2016c) *Autumn Statement 2016*, Cm 9362, November.

Holt, A. (2015) *Outsourcing services in local government: The West Sussex experience*, July, London: Unison.

House of Commons (2011) *Localism*, Communities and Local Government Select Committee Report, 7 June.

House of Commons (2013a) *Blacklisting in employment: Interim report*, Scottish Affairs Committee, March.

House of Commons (2013b) *Police and Crime Commissioners*, Home Affairs Committee, May.

House of Commons (2013c) *Department for Communities and Local Government: Financial sustainability of local authorities*, Committee of Public Accounts, 4 June.

House of Commons (2015a) *Statutory Instruments Public Procurement 2015*, No 102, 4 February.

House of Commons (2015b) *Devolving responsibilities to cities in England: Wave 1 City Deals*, Committee of Public Accounts, November.

House of Commons Library (2014) 'Local elections 2014', Research Paper 14/33.

House of Commons Library (2015) 'Local elections 2015', Briefing Paper No CBP7204.

House of Commons Library (2016a) 'Local elections 2016', Briefing Paper No CBP7596.

House of Commons Library (2016b) 'London elections 2016', Briefing Paper No CBP7598.

House of Commons Library (2016c) 'National Assembly for Wales elections: 2016', Briefing Paper NumNober CBP7594.

House of Commons Library (2016d) 'Scottish Parliament elections: 2016', Briefing Paper No CBP7599.

House of Commons Library (2016e) 'Comparison of Right to Buy policies in England, Scotland, Wales and Northern Ireland', Briefing Paper No 07174.

House of Commons Library (2016f) 'Local government: alternative models of service delivery', Briefing Paper No 05950.

House of Commons Library (2016g) 'Membership of UK political parties', Briefing Paper No SN05125.

Innes, D. and Tetlow, G. (2015) 'Delivering Fiscal Squeeze by Cutting Local Government Spending', Institute of Fiscal Studies, 15 September.

Johnson, P. (2015) 'Summer post-Budget briefing', 9 July, http://www.ifs.org.uk/search?q=Budget+July+2015.

Jones, G. (2010) 'The Coalition government's "new localism" decentralisation agenda may well undermine local government. A new agreement is needed', 22 November, http://blogs.lse.ac.uk/politicsandpolicy/archives/5615.

Jones, G. (2012) 'Elected mayors cannot deliver a localist revival', 20 April, http://blogs.lse.ac.uk/politicsandpolicy/elected-mayors-localism-jones/.

Jones, G. and Stewart, J. (2012) 'Reflections on the Localism Act', in *The world will be your oyster?* Birmingham: INLOGOV, pp 94–9.

Labour Land Campaign (2011) *Manifesto*, http://www.labourland.org/.

Labour Party (2015) *Britain can be better: The Labour Party manifesto 2015*, 13 April, London.

Labour Representation Committee (2015) 'Bring a new politics into local democracy', *Campaign News*, 21 December.

Latham, P. (2011a) *The state and local government: Towards a new basis for 'local democracy' and the defeat of big business control*, Croydon: Manifesto Press.

Latham, P. (2011b) 'Land Value Taxation, debt and human rights: A Gramscian perspective', *Accountancy Business and the Public Interest*, vol 10, pp 94–123.

Latham, P. (2014) 'No plan B: should Croydon pin its hopes on Westfield?', *Croydon Citizen*, 25 November.

Latham, P. (2015) 'Reverting to the committee system: why and how', briefing paper prepared for the National Pensioners Convention, Greater London Regional Council, 26 June.

Local Government Association (2011) *Police and crime panels: Guidance on role and composition*, London: LGA.

McCulloch, N. and Pacillo, G. (2011) *The Tobin Tax: A review of the evidence*, Institute of Development Studies, Research Report 68, May, Brighton: IDS.

McKenna, H. and Dunn, P. (2015) *Devolution: What it means for health and social care in England*, Briefing, The King's Fund Briefing, November.

Mirrlees, J. (ed) (2011) *Tax by design: The Mirrlees Review*, September, Oxford: Oxford University Press.

Nandy, L., Lucas, C. and Bowers, C. (eds) (2016) *The Alternative: Towards a new progressive politics*, London: Biteback Publising.

NAO (National Audit Office) (2014) *Financial sustainability of local authorities 2014*, 19 November, London: NAO.

NAO (2016) *English devolution deals*, HC 948, 20 April, London: NAO.

NCIA (National Coalition for Independent Action) (2011) *Voluntary action under threat: What privatisation means for charities and community groups*, May, London: NCIA.

Needham, R. (2016) 'Participatory budgeting a school for citizenship', 27 April, http://lawcha.org/wordpress/2016/04/27/participatory-budgeting-school-citizenship/.

NILGA (Northern Ireland Local Government Association) (2015) *Councillors's guide*, Belfast: NILGA.

OBR (Office for Budget Responsibility) (2014) *Economic and fiscal outlook*, December, London: OBR.

OBR (2015) *Economic and fiscal outlook,* July, London: OBR.

ONS (Office of National Statistics) (2015a) 'Public sector employment Q1 2015', *Statistical Bulletin*, 17 June, London: ONS.

Piketty, T. (2014a) 'Dynamics of inequality', *New Left Review* 85, second series, January/February, pp 103–16.

Piketty, T. (2014b) *Capital in the twenty-first century*, Kindle edition, London: Harvard University.

PWC (PricewaterhouseCoopers LLP) (2014) *Best value inspection of London Borough of Tower Hamlets report*, London: PWC.

PWC (2015) *Delivering the decentralisation dividend: A whole system approach*, London: PWC.

Rallings, C. and Thrasher, M. (2013) 'The 2012 Police and Crime Commissioner elections in England and Wales: aspects of participation and administration', University of Plymouth.

Rallings, C., Thrasher, M. and Cowling, D. (2012) 'Mayoral referendums and elections: uninterested electors and unknowing voters', paper presented to Elections, Public Opinion and Parties Annual Conference, University of Oxford, 7–9 September, pp 1–25.

Rallings, C., Thrasher, M. and Cowling, D. (2014) 'Mayoral referendums and elections revisited', *British Politics*, vol 9, pp 2–28.

Reeves, A., Basu, S., McKee, M., Marmot, M. and Stuckler, M. (2013) 'Austere or not? UK coalition government budgets and health inequalities', *Journal of the Royal Society of Medicine*, 11 September, pp 1–5.

Roche, A. (2015) Unison briefing calling for delay of the UK Public Contracts Regulations 2015, 26 February.

Roth, O. (2010) *A fair cop? Elected police commissioners, democracy and local accountability*, London: New Local Government Network.

Salveson, P. (2015) 'A case for regional parliaments?' *Chartist*, January/February, p 7.

STUC (Scottish TUC and Scottish CND) (2015) *Trident and jobs: The case for a Scottish defence diversification agency*, April.

Shelter (2015) 'Housing and Planning Bill: second reading briefing', October.

Sikka, P. (2011) 'Reverse socialism', *Chartist*, May/June, p 9.

Smyth, S. and Whitfield, D. (2016/forthcoming) 'Maintaining market principles: government auditors, PPP equity sales and hegemony', *Accounting Forum*, http://dx.doi.org/10.1016/j.accfor.2016.06.003.

Stevens, Lord (Chair) (2013) *Policing for a better Britain*, London: Report of the Independent Police Commission.

Streeck, W. (2014) 'How will capitalism end?' *New Left Review*, 87, second series, May/June, pp 35–64.

TUC and NEF (Trades Union Congress and the New Economics Foundation) (2015) *Outsourcing public services*, London: New Economics Foundation.

Wainwright, S. (2016) 'Radicalising the party-movement relationship: from Ralph Miliband to Jeremy Corbyn and beyond', in L. Panitch and G. Albo (eds) *Socialist Register 2017*, pp 80–101, London: The Merlin Press.

Watkins, S. (2016) 'Casting off?' *New Left Review*, 100, second series, July/August, pp 5–31.

Whitfield, D. (2014) *UK outsourcing expands despite high failure rates*, PPP Database, Strategic Partnerships 2012–2013, January.

Whitfield, D. (2015) *Alternative to private finance of the welfare state: A global analysis of social impact bond, pay-for-success and development bond projects*, South Australia: The University of Adelaide.

Whitfield, D. (2016) 'The financial commodification of public infrastructure: the growth of offshore secondary market infrastructure funds', October.

Williams, Z. (2012) *The shadow state: A report about outsourcing of public services*, London: Social Enterprise UK.

Index

References to tables are in *italics*